The Heathen's Guide to Christmas

By William Hopper

Original art , design, illustration ©copyright 2008 by
William Hopper
Cover design by William Hopper
Editing assistance gratefully accepted from:
Wilson Fowlie and M. Terese Hopper
An Eris book

Table of Contents

Christmas, 1971

The year had been a hard one. Evil nuns with yardsticks and rosary beads ruled my life back then, making sure that I learned all there was to know about Curious George and keeping quiet in class. It was the latter that I had the most problem with, and by late October I had the strap marks to prove it.

But this was December; Christmas. I had been good for almost two full months, and I knew it was all about to pay off. Hours of diligent homework, doing chores, and being polite were about to net me the greatest treasure I could ever think of: the Jonny Lightning Racer Set. The mall Santa fully alerted, my family appropriately hinted at, I went to bed Christmas Eve confident that the next morning would be the fulfillment of all those months of dreaming and hoping.

Eight hours and an eternity later, my brothers and I stood in front of that huge blue spruce, waiting while my father meted out the gifts left by one S. Claus. Being the youngest I waited the longest, patiently biding my time while my gift made its way to the top of the pile. The card had barely been read before I launched myself, tearing for all I was worth at the red and green wrapping that stood between me and...

...Plasticine.

I'd never seen Plasticine before. To me, at that moment, the box with four colored strips of clay was tantamount to coal in my stocking. What had I done wrong? Why was I being punished? Where was my Johnny Lightning Racer Set? Hadn't ANYONE bothered to pay attention to my homework? My behavior? The thousand hints I'd dropped every chance I could get? I wanted to scream. I wanted to lash out at a world I was beginning to understand was cruel and unfair. Plasticine! What good was Plasticine when there were Johnny Lightning Racer Sets in the world!?!

Outwardly, I showed no sign of this torment. I smiled and walked off to play with this new goop, pretending to be happy with it all. But when no one was looking I just sat there staring at that Plasticine, mourning the bright red and green wrap that had held so much promise an hour earlier. It wasn't fair. A grievous error had been made here, and I was the innocent victim of it. Someone would be punished. Someone HAD to be punished. But who?

Then it came to me. Like a beacon of light through the mesh of torn wrapping, the card shone forth, exposing his guilt for the whole world to see:

"S. Claus".

"That fat bastard's gonna pay." I promised myself. "I can't get him yet, but someday, SOMEDAY, that twisted little imp is going to get what's coming to him. He *will* pay..."

And so, with no further ado, I welcome you to *The Heathen's Guide To Christmas*.

Wm. Hopper

Chapter One: Beware of Dog

The test of a good religion is whether or not you can joke about it. ~G.K. Chesterton

When I was young I had a dog named Chuck. Although I learned to love him dearly, it didn't take long to figure out that, as loyal and cute as Chuck was, he had the IQ of a rhododendron.

I lived in a sixth-floor apartment at the time, and we'd often take the elevator down to the ground level to allow Chuck to do his thing. Dense as he was, it took no time at all for him to realize that getting on the elevator meant that he'd be able to run free when it got to the bottom. As soon as the doors parted, he'd tear off, bound for the grass at the other end of the parking lot. This worked extremely well... on the ground floor.

The problems occurred when the elevator was forced to stop at, say, the third floor. Chuck, not understanding the complexities of elevator mechanics, would tear out with the same enthusiasm, careening into the opposite wall with a heavy, dull thud. Try as we might, we could never break him of this habit. You could hold him as tight as you wanted, but as soon as that door opened, he was gone. On any floor but the bottom one, he'd slam face first into the wall opposite.

Somehow I'm reminded of old Chuck as I begin this book. Looking over the vast array of data in front of me, I can't help but wonder at how these Christmas myths have stayed alive over the years. In my kinder moments I tend to think of the sheep that buy into this Christmas farce as being like Chuck: Well intentioned, but always encountering a brick wall because they haven't quite grasped the mechanics of history. I figure, like Chuck, they have their eye on the world the way they want it to be, ignoring anything that might alter this vision.

Now, this may be an ok way to look at life. I mean, if people want to believe in the traditional Santa Claus myth, the Nativity story, and all the window dressing that go with it, perhaps they're happier that way. After all, who am I to tell them they're wrong? Ignorance is bliss, as they say, and the information I have in front of me is certainly going to tear apart a lot of the foundations of the Christmas myth. I suppose I really have to stop at some point and ask myself "Do I really have the right to destroy the joyous ignorance that religions and marketing boards have worked so hard to create for these people?" Chuck, after all, lived a happy life.

In the end, though, I can't help thinking of how happy Chuck looked the day he chased that squirrel into oncoming traffic, killing himself and sending the car and its driver smashing into a nearby lamp post. This in mind, I think it's about time we got started...

The Nativity: An Infantile Beginning...

'I wanted to give birth as opposed to being delivered.' ~ Ricki Lake

Let's start with a little game of Virgin Birth. Here's the way it works: find someone who's pro-Christian/pro-Christmas. After assuring them that you're not going to offend them with a bit of historical fact (lie) read the following bits out loud and ask them to guess who you're talking about. You get one point for pissing them off, five points for being told you're going to hell, and 25 points (and a mention on my website) if they actually haul off and hit you.

Scenario One:

Born on December 25 to a virgin mother, this great man later sacrificed his life so he could save all humanity from eternal torment. He died at Easter of acute crucifixion, and descended for three days into the underworld. On Easter Sunday, he rose again. To commemorate this heroic story, his followers wore an image of him being crucified and he was symbolically eaten by his followers in the form of bread during services.

Answer: Attis, a Phrygian god from Asia Minor. If anyone said Jesus, point your finger, laugh, and sign yourself up for 5 points. That one was pretty obscure though. To be fair, let's jump ahead a bit to the actual time of Jesus.

Scenario Two:

He was worshipped in Jerusalem in the 1st century. He was the Son of God. The Creator made his mother pregnant through mystic means and his flesh and blood were symbolically eaten in the form of bread and wine by his devotees to celebrate his birth on December 25. The guy's into healing, saving your soul, and eternal love. Oh... and a star appeared above when he was born. Don't forget to mention the star.

Answer: Dionysus, the son of Zeus. Dionysian worship was really big in Rome and all the territories that Rome controlled, including Israel/Judea.

Ok, let's try this one on for size...

Scenario Three:

A savior-god called the Lord of Lords, King of Kings, God of Gods. He is the

Resurrection and the Life, the Good Shepherd, yadda yadda, (you get the idea). Three Wise Men announced his birth. His followers ate cakes of wheat that symbolized his body, and he was worshipped in Judea in the first century AD.

Answer: That one's Osiris, the Egyptian God who was chopped into 14 pieces as a sacrifice for all humanity. The difference between his lore and Jesus' is that when Osiris came back from the dead, when Isis helped him out, she couldn't (or wouldn't) find his penis. For this reason Osiris is generally portrayed as neutered. Rome had accepted Osiris into the Hall of Gods by the time of Jesus, and Osiris worship was an accepted practice under Rome's Hellenism. (Hellenism, by the way, was kind of a syncretic mish-mash of all the gods into one religion. Syncretic, by the way, is just a big word for mish-mash.)

Ok... that's three virgin births and three resurrections, and we're still not up to the late great JC.
Here comes my favorite...

Scenario Four:
A guy born of a virgin on December 25 (popular day for virgin births, huh?). As an adult he casts out demons, cures people and walks on water. He was killed to save all humanity, came

back from the dead, then ascended into heaven. He'll come again to judge the living and the dead and his kingdom will have no end.

Answer: Mithras, the god of Mithraism (also associated with Zoroastrianism). It was from this religion that Christianity stole the bulk of its lore. Mithras was the Sol Invictus or Unconquerable Sun. He did battle on behalf of humanity, died a martyr, and rose again. His story comes complete with 12 apostles, a Last Supper, the Wise Men and the Shepherds bit. His Godly Father, Ahura Mazda, was the One True God (except for that other pesky god he kept having trouble with.)

Ok, tally up your score and see how you did. If you're bleeding or incapable of writing because you've just had your hands broken, don't bother counting it all up. You win automatically.

Virgin Territory

"Losing your faith is a lot like losing your virginity, you don't realize how irritating it was 'til it's gone" ~ Madonna

Ok, this is been fun, but I suppose I should make an attempt to explain what the hell I'm talking about. All these references to old religions seem really irrelevant these days, but there was a time when they were pivotal. You see, Christianity was not born in a vacuum. The religion came into being at a time when the Roman Empire was at its height. Dozens of countries had been amalgamated (slaughtered) into one giant dominion, and the culture of Rome reflected the diversity of its people. Sure, we're all told about the opulence of Rome before the rise of Christianity: the feasting and orgies and naked revelers frolicking in the streets (ah, the good old days...). What the religious folks tend to forget is that these cults provided Christianity with many of its myths, especially those that relate to Christmas.

The nativity tale you find in the Bible is really just a myth that was built up in several different religions at the time. It worked kind of like an urban legend; the general story was there in a bunch of different faiths, but the names and places varied depending on who was telling the story. You don't have to just blindly believe me on this one. I'll quote it to you directly from the Catholic Encyclopedia Online, under the heading Mithraism, just in case you happen to run into some priest who says he's never heard of such a thing.

"Mithras is called a mediator; and so is Christ. Mithraism had a Eucharist as Christ did; a last supper before his sacrifice. Mithras saved the world by sacrificing a bull; Christ by sacrificing Himself. Both Mithras and Christ are born of divine plan and intervention."

If you read on in the encyclopedia, the guy that wrote it claims that Mithraism stole from Christianity. He seems to neglect to mention that the Mithras story is about 2000 years older than the Jesus story. If you doubt this, look it up. The Mithras tale evolved from the Rig Veda (a Hindu holy book) written somewhere around 5000BC by the Vedics. You can find both the Rig Veda and the Catholic Encyclopedia in your local library or on-line. Also, check out stuff by Asclepius, or pretty much anything written at the time by Pliny, Josephus or even the Greek guy, Herodotus. They all give a smattering of info about the festivals of Mithras et al.

The Holy Bible

No man ever believes that the Bible means what it says: He is always convinced that it says what he means. ~George Bernard Shaw

The fact that I'm using Biblical references here should not be seen as my putting any stock whatsoever in the Bible. However, I figure if I'm dealing with the Christians on the Christmas story I'd better be able to fight them on their own turf. Besides, what kind of guide to Heathenism would I be if I couldn't give you enough ammo to hit your Christian opponents where they live and breathe: The Holy Word of God. So, in mid-rant over this whole virgin birth thing, I suggest you resort to shock tactics and pull out the Bible. Here are some handy verses you can throw at them next time they get to telling you how Christian this holiday season is.

Ok... two guys, Mark and John, wrote books that recounted the many and varied spectacles of the Son of God's life here on Earth. The whole crucifixion and resurrection story's in there, as are the other major events in the life of Jesus. But it seems that these devout chroniclers of the life of the Divine Son of God had never heard of the Virgin Birth Story. Check it out for yourself: it ain't there. No wise men, no angels, no mention of God coming down to impregnate Jesus' mom, no donkey ride to Bethlehem. As far as Mark and John were concerned, there was nothing worth reporting about the birth of Jesus. They each start their tale when Jesus was older and starting to preach.

Now, you'd figure that somewhere along the line that they might have been tipped off that Jesus was born of the mating of a God and a virgin, but apparently not. I figure either the Virgin Birth story was added to Christianity later than these gospels, or the other apostles just kept the virgin tale a secret from Mark and John, preferring instead to point and snicker at them behind their backs when they tried to tell Jesus' life story.

These two books, the gospels of John and Mark, make up half of the total knowledge we have of the life of JC. This leaves us only the stories of Matthew and Luke to rely on to discover the true meaning of Christmas.

Suddenly I feel like Jimmy Stewart.

The Virgin

Mothers are fonder of their children than fathers because they are more certain they are their own. ~ Aristotle

Ok, we'd all like to find a virgin, and the Christians are no exception. But, as has happened SO many times in my life, the story never quite fits the facts. My apologies about this, but I have to throw a few Bible references at you on this whole virgin idea. I figure I'd better give them to you because as soon as you start telling anyone about this whole virgin "misconception" they're gonna want you to prove it. So, here are the proofs...

In the first chapter of Matthew's book, (verse 22 for the biblical scholars out there) Matt talks about an Old Testament prophesy. The bit he's referring to is in the Book of Isaiah. The thing is, Matt was reading a Greek translation of Isaiah (which was originally written in Hebrew.) Now, we don't have the book that Matt was working from, but we do know from the way he talked about it that whoever did the translation from Hebrew to Greek screwed it up. Among other things, the translation Matt had for the Hebrew word Bethulah, was wrong. The translator had said the word meant "virgin", which is where we get the idea of Mary being a virgin when JC was born. The thing is, it should have said "young woman." The Isaiah bit in question was a prophecy about the new king that was to show up. We know the word's supposed to be "young woman" (not "virgin") because most of the copies available in Jewish synagogues today are still in the original Hebrew and the word clearly means "young woman" in Hebrew. It was Matt's Greek version of the Isaiah prophesy that was translated wrong, and he used the translation to back up the Virgin Birth tale. Ok... it's not that fascinating a story. But it does start to explain where a lot of this comes from.

The Magi

Believe those who are seeking the truth; doubt those who find it. ~ Andre Gide

Now, for those who have a special hatred for the Three Wise Men (also called "the Magi" by eggheads) that always sit off to the side in those cheesy, plaster Nativity scenes, I have some good news for you: they were never there. That's right... they never made it to the birth scene according to the Bible story.

According to the Bible, Herod asked the Magi for the exact time that the star appeared so he could learn exactly when Jesus was born. As the Magi contended that they were looking for a "new king", Herod supposedly set to having all the kids who were born at the correct time executed so that they never threatened his reign. (I think this story is BS by the way. Nowhere else but in the Xian story do you hear about Herod killing thousands of kids. A story like that would have definitely been recorded by at least one of the scribes of the day, and for generations afterwards.) As this death order supposedly went out for any child under 2 years of age, JC could have been living with his parents in Bethlehem for somewhere up to two years by the time that the Magi arrived. You see, if the Magi were part of the Nativity story that would mean that JC was just born, so Herod would have ordered only newborns killed.

The Magi's absence from the nativity tale pretty much calls into question the whole idea of giving gifts at Christmas as a remembrance of the gold, frankincense, and myrrh they supposedly gave Jesus. As the Magi weren't actually there at the time he was born (if, indeed, any of this story is true at all) the Christian explanation for gift giving seems to fall by the wayside. You might want to point this out to your Christian friends... after you get the gifts of course.

Anyway... In Matthew 2:9, the bit about the Magi following a star to the exact location in the manger where JC was supposedly born is obviously mythical. Any comet or star that was that close enough to pinpoint for them the exact location of one manger in the middle of a town would incinerate it in a second.

By the way, all of these questions were readily answered by the Apostle Peter in his Gospel, wherein he intricately traces the virgin birth, the star bit, and the Magi. You may not have heard of this particular gospel, but Pete goes into great detail about the childhood of Jesus (i.e.: the "missing years") wherein he talks about the miracles Jesus did as a boy. He chronicles things like Jesus making doves in the sand then waving his hand over them and having them come to life, or killing a bunch of kids by calling their names and they dropped dead on the spot (they were teasing him at the time.) Anyway, the Gospel of Peter could have answered all the questions we have about the nativity tale. I say "could have." The book still exists, but even the Christians weren't stupid enough to try to pass these stories off as authentic.

The Census

Mary and Joseph supposedly travelled on a donkey to go to Bethlehem because Rome had ordered a census. Aside from the fact that this whole story was stolen from Attis worship (his mother also did the donkey ride thing to have a virgin birth in a strange town) there are a few logistical problems here. Even if a census did happen at the time the Bible says it did (which I doubt since we don't have any independent record of a census at the time), I can't see why Rome would care about the people returning to the city in which they were born. I could see Rome wanting an accurate head count for taxation purposes, but I can't see why they'd care where the people were when they were counted. Besides, as only men were taxed back then, there'd be no reason for Joseph to drag his pregnant wife with him all the way.

The Shepherds

In Chislev, the Hebrew month corresponding to October, the shepherds would move their flocks inside and tend them in barns for the winter. (By the way, a manger, like the one the Late Great JC was supposedly born in, is a trough for feeding cattle.) By Bul, the month that corresponds to December, the flocks were inside all the time, mainly because it was just too damn cold for the shepherds to be "abiding in the field" as old Luke there said they were. Come December, these guys would have been freezing their butts off in the field. If you read the Nativity tale, you'll see that Luke makes no mention of these guys freezing their butts off.

The Date

In 245 AD (while Christianity was still illegal in Rome) a bunch of Christians decided they wanted to figure out the exact date of Jesus' birth. The Church fathers, led at the time by Origen, decreed that it would be a sin to celebrate the birth of Jesus "as though he were a King Pharaoh." (Quoted directly from Panati's Extraordinary Origins, Page 33.) It seems the Church Fathers wanted to keep the Jesus stuff as far away from the Roman celebrations as they could. They of course failed, but at least they managed to stave off the inevitable for 80 years until the Council of Nicaea in 325.

I'm gonna go out on a limb on this one and guess that no one wants to hear about ecumenical councils in the fourth century, so I'm gonna skip the dreary history lesson and get on with the actual date thing....

The Month

Shepherds were not out in the fields in December. According to the bible, they were in the plains when the angels appeared to them, which means they were either on their way up to the higher grasslands, or coming back down. This means the angels had to have appeared in either mid-spring or mid-autumn. In summer they were in the mountains, and in the winter the shepherds would have been back near the cities where they could feed the livestock from stored grain. Accordingly, Jesus would have had to be born in the spring or autumn according to the angel story. This is assuming you accept the idea of flying messengers from God showing up in the middle of the night to sing to a bunch of guys watching sheep. I tend to be a tad skeptical.

The Year

We say JC was born in 1 AD. It's the AD part that works it that way. AD stands for "anno domini", which just means "year of our Lord." The whole AD and BC thing was created by a monk named Dionysius Exigus in the sixth century. Charlemagne, one of the greatest blood-thirsty conquerors of all time, adopted Dionysius' calendar long after he came up with it and it's been pretty much accepted ever since.

It was this Dionysius guy who supposedly made December 25 the official day of the Christ Mass (Christmas) and declared that the Nativity story happened on that day. (Note: He was named after one of the big gods of Hellenism, Dionysius. I only tell you this so that no one looks at you and says "Hey, Dionysius was a god, not a monk!" Those Christians can be well informed in their fanaticism.)

The thing is, Dionysus was working from the old calendar, which used Anno Urbis, or year of the city of Rome. All Dionysus did was translate the old calendar into the new one and set up Jesus' birth as Year One. Pretty much everyone who's looked over this guy's work agrees that he screwed up by at least four years. By the Roman records we have, JC was born in 750 AU, or 4 BC. So Dionysus was off by about four years.

The Hebrew Christmas Tree

Read the following chapter and verse aloud when sitting with friends and family around the Christmas tree. It ought to set the mood nicely. It's Jeremiah 10, verse three for those that have to actually prove it to someone. Here we go... the first biblical Christmas tree reference:

Thus says the LORD: "Learn not the ways of the nations, for the customs of the peoples are false. A tree from the forest is cut down...men deck it with silver and gold; they fasten it with hammer and nails so that it cannot move."

That's from Jeremiah's time... about the time the Babylonian invasion of Israel. King Nebuchadnezzar had slaughtered a whole bunch of them and taken the survivors off to Babylon to be slaves. This whole anti-Christmas tree declaration was Jeremiah's way of trying to keep the Israelites from adopting a bunch of pagan beliefs into the mythos of Yahweh. He didn't like this whole business of taking a tree from the forest and decorating it with silver and gold because it was a ritual from a Baal religion. (oh... "Baal." It means "Lord" and refers to the small gods or goddesses that were so prolific in the desert back then. Kind of like genies. Baal generally looked over one city or one area.) Marduk, the Baal of Babylon, was the guy the tree ceremony was originally intended to honor. The Jews, spurred by Jeremiah's devotion and condemnation, utterly rejected this idea and would never, ever adopt such a foreign element into their religion. They left that to the Christians a couple hundred years later.

Xmas

I love this whole "Xmas" versus "Christmas" debate. Modern "Xians" resent us heathenous slime using an X instead of the title "Christ" in words like Xmas or Xian. They say this is an affront to Jesus and an attempt to take the Christ out of Christmas. While I don't see any real problem with that goal, I love pointing out to these guys that the X used to replace the word Christ was invented by the Catholics, not the atheists. The idea here is that the X is supposed to look like the cross on which Jesus was sacrificed. So, by putting the X there, you're constantly reminding the people of the horrible sacrifice Jesus supposedly made on Calvary. Names like Christopher and Christine were often spelled with the X instead of the Christ part in baptismal and marriage certificates as homage to Jesus' crucifixion.

The thing is, most Christians out there never bother to educate themselves on their own history before they go out screaming and yelling at people for maligning it. When modern Christians see this monogram, they believed it HAD to be a slight to their faith. However much the secularists might like to take the credit for it, the X was a Christian invention. Please, as a favor to me, point this out next time you're sitting around and someone starts complaining about taking the Christ out of Christmas.

The Making of Christmas

Christmas? There are much worse thing to believe in. ~Steven Colbert

Ok, I've been trashing the Christian side of the Christmas story so far, but I figure it's about time I started explaining where a lot of this stuff actually came from.

Christmas is really just a bunch of religious myths and festivals stolen from a bunch of different religions and stuffed into Christian lore. You see, when Emperor Constantine (300-329AD) and those that came after him put this Christmas thing together they just took the festivals that already existed in Rome, dumped the god they were designed for, then inserted Jesus as the top guy. Here's a quick list of the religious holidays they stole from:

The biggest Roman feast of the year was called Saturnalia on December 25. Before Constantine it was officially a festival for Saturn. Here's the playlist of what went on in December throughout the Roman Empire (including Israel/Jerusalem) until the fourth century AD. These are only the official holidays that you can readily read about in works by Josephus, Pliny the Elder, Horas, Cicero, et al.

- Saturn's Feast, December 25:

- Ops (Goddess of plenty/agriculture), December 19.
- Consualia, end of sowing season festival, December 15.
- Dies Juvenalis, Coming of Age for Young Men, December 22
- Feast of Mithras, the Unconquerable Sun, December 25
- Brumalia, Winter Solstice on pre-Julian calendar, December 25.
- Janus Day and New Year's, January 1

You'll note they don't all fall on December 25. This is where the idea of the Twelve Days of Christmas comes from. In Rome, the season started somewhere around the 15th and carried through to January 1. The Christians, in adopting all this, kept the idea of a "season" of festivals (reduced to 12 days) but chucked out all the gods and goddesses that were supposed to be honored on the various days.

All these feasts predate Christmas by a long shot, and are centered on what the Romans called the Winter Solstice, or Yule. I better cover that whole Solstice thing before we go much further because it's pretty much the reason we have Christmas in the first place...

Solstice

The word solstice means "sun standing still". It's an astronomy thing. You see, the winter solstice that they called Saturnalia became the "birthday" of several gods: Adonis, Zeus, Odin etc.. It's a "solar birthday," marking the time that the sun is at its weakest point, like a newborn child. The Romans celebrated the birth of the gods on this day. After the solstice, as the days began to get longer, the people thought that the sun gods were getting stronger and they saw this as the god getting older and growing up. A real deep philosophy that one...

The reality of the situation, by the way, is exactly the opposite. The Earth is closer to the sun in January than it is in June. The seasons aren't caused by the distance from the sun, but by the angle of the Earth. The planet leans 23 degrees and 27 minutes off the proper orbit, making one side or the other of the planet lean more towards the sun. Which side depends on where you are in our orbit around the sun. Sometimes it's summer in New Zealand, sometimes in the States. It depends on what part of the earth is leaning toward the sun at that time of year. The actual distance from the sun is irrelevant. Being off by a million miles here or there to something that big doesn't affect the amount of radiation we get. It's only the angle that makes it seem stronger or weaker. Granted, this all sounds like a grade 10 science lesson, but I figured I'd throw it in just so you can get an idea of the reality in the face of all the "mystic solstice" stuff we've been covering.

I have no idea how long ago humans figured all this solstice stuff out, but I gotta admit it was pretty ingenious. Somehow or other these guys managed to look around them and figure out the rotation of the planets, the speed of the orbits, and the times of the various astronomical events. Using all this data, they were able to work out to the minute when the shortest and longest days occurred, which was pretty damned impressive without calculators, satellites, or computers.

Bringing It All Together...

There is no need for temples; no need for complicated philosophy. Our own brain, our own heart is our temple; the philosophy is kindness. ~The Dalai Lama

A whole bunch of religions (like the Marduk thing with the Christmas tree) had all merged into one big religion called Hellenism under Alexander the Great. By the time of Jesus, Rome had won back all the territory that Alexander had conquered, and all the gods they came across were worshipped in Rome under this one religion called Hellenism. It's what the Caesars and Emperors all believed in, and what the Saturnalia celebrations in Rome were about.

I'd be pretty remiss to say that this whole Hellenism thing is the entire origin of Christmas though. It took centuries of fine manipulation and politics to create the annoying holiday we all know and hate. We can pretty much accept that the Virgin Birth story and the date of Christmas, December 25, come from Rome and the solstice celebrations. But this is only the foundation of the crap. It took centuries of political and religious crap to turn these simple festivals into the schlocky, mass-marketed tripe that leaves you broke and miserable every January.

The next step in the evolution of this tripe comes from the rise of the Holy Roman Catholic Church, and its desperate attempts to control the people and lands of Europe.

Catholic Christmas

The Roman Catholic Church officially became a political body on January 1, 800 AD. That's the date most historians give for the start of the Holy Roman Catholic Empire, when the popes finally ousted enough of the emperors of Europe to say they ran the place. Practically, though, this date is about 400 years too late. Christianity really got its political power during the reign of Constantine in 300-336 AD. Guys like Augustine and Bernard of Clairvox solidified this power over the next couple centuries, but it was effectively there when the emperor Constantine adopted the faith for his reign.

The whole reason the Roman Catholic Empire came into being in 800 AD is because the popes systematically manipulated or killed any opposition to their new religion throughout all of Europe from 300 to 800 AD. What they couldn't kill off, they adopted into the religion so they could maintain control. This had absolutely nothing to do with maintaining any kind of religious integrity... it was about politics and tithes.

You see, the old Roman Empire was crumbling at the time, and there was a real battle going on in Europe to see who would emerge as the political and religious victor. The popes had the most power because of Constantine, but even they had no guarantee of coming out of this era alive, let alone in power. There were a lot of rival religions and cultures around that were battling for the same lands, and only the most bloodthirsty, manipulative, and cruel could ever hope to survive. In the end, the Christians won hands down.

This win was not without its concessions though. Rome was confronted with a lot of opposition, and some of it was just as cruel, powerful, and bloody as they were. Case in point: the Celts. These guys had a long history of being the best damned invading army the Mediterranean had ever seen. So, when Rome went off to convert their homeland in Britannia and Ireland, they had to convert these heathenous, pagan people the only way they could. Instead of trying to get them to give up their religion, they decided to take the taxes instead and not give a damn about the religion.

The Celts had to accept Christianity in name only, so long as they militarily and financially supported Rome in every other regard. After being assured that the Roman rule would in no way effect the sanctity of their religion or, more importantly, their whiskey, accepted this. To explain how this happened and why Rome was so worried about the Celts, I gotta cover all the torture, mayhem, and carnage that preceded this era. This, I hope, will in some small way make up for all the damn bible references earlier.

Norse and Celts

Do not give up the religion of your youth until you get a better one. ~Martin H. Fischer

The Norse and Celts had military cultures. They'd kill anything that fought back and rape anything that didn't. (It didn't pay to be a pacifist when the Norse came to town.). There's this modern misconception that the Celts were kindly, earthy people that lived in the woods of Ireland, ate potatoes, and danced lively gigs with elves and leprechauns. Indeed, some Celts actually did live this way, but it really depended on what they were smoking in their pipes at the time. For the vast majority of their history, however, the Celts were not a peaceable folk. In fact, they were exactly the viscous, cruel, and blood-thirsty type of culture that makes all this so much fun to study. Let me show you what Rome was really up against when they decided to convert Ireland and Britannia...

The earliest archaeological signs we have of the Celts starts around 1200 BC., during the Iron Age. They moved into the British Isles somewhere around 400 BC, and started a-killing . By the time of Jesus, these guys had butchered someone from basically every settlement in Europe, as far away as Sicily, Greece, and even Turkey. They had a pretty good name for themselves as marauders, and even the Greeks learned to keep away from them. We get the name Celts from the Greeks. Herodotus, one of my favorite Greek writers, called the Celts "Keltoi" which loosely translates as "that bastard just stabbed me with an IRON dagger!!!". (The Celts were the original guys to refine iron into useful weapons and tools) The Romans called the Celts Galli, or Gauls.

Anyway, these guys were pretty damned good. In their early history they conquered Italy, sacked Rome in 390 BC, looted Macedonia in 279 BC, and killed most of the population of Thessaly. The chronicles of their sacking of the Oracle at Delphi stands in the history books as one of the most brutal affronts ever. (An oracle is a natural temple... usually built into a mountain side or lake or something) I mean, these guys walked into Greece, one of the most defensive and military cultures of the day, and managed to destroy the most important religious and cultural center in the country. You always hear about the Trojan war the Greeks had with the Turks, but this was way better. I figure there's so little record of it because the Greeks just hate to be reminded of what the Celts did to their country.

Anyway, you get the idea. The Celts that the Romans encountered when they took over Ireland were not some small band of happy-go-lucky potato farmers. They were the descendants of a people who had actually conquered Rome at one time, and the popes knew it. There was no way they were going to go in there with swords blazing trying to beat the Celts into submission. They might have been able to do it, but the cost in manpower and money would never have been worth it. It was better take over with open arms, doing so as quietly and peaceably as they could.

This is where the story of St. Patrick comes in... He was one of the Christian missionaries who "converted" Ireland in the 5th century AD. He was a Catholic missionary sent in to convert these people. Before he got there, Rome had already proved it was now militarily stronger than the Celts (It had been about 700 years since the Celts invaded Rome).

Still, St. Patrick and his Christian ilk were well aware that these people had a history. So, when establishing the dominion of Christianity over Ireland and Britannia, they didn't really push too hard, especially where celebrations and festivals were concerned. It was best to leave them as much of their own culture as possible, while setting things up so the political and economic control of the region was governed by Rome. The result was a whole lot of "additions" to the Christmas tale that were suspiciously similar (i.e.: exactly the same as) as the pagan festivals the Celts had before the Romans got there.

When Rome encountered the Norsemen (the Vikings) a few hundred years later, they employed the exact same strategy, thus adding even further to the deep meaning of Christmas. None of which, you'll notice, has anything what so ever to do with the late great JC. Kinda liking that part of it all...

It's Beginning to Look A Lot Like Christmas

Ok, here's where it all starts to look more like the annoying Christmas we see today...

A lot of the modern God mythos comes from the Celts and Norse, including the name God. It comes from the Norse word Ghuto, or gydig. Both words mean "the called" or "the invoked." All the other names of God, like Elohim and Yahweh, all come from Hebrew. But the common name, God, is actually a Norse word. For our purposes the name God comes from the Norse word Ghuto meaning "the invoked." It actually also means the giddy, but we won't get into the implications of that. Apparently I have to keep this book at a PG 13 reading level.

Anyway, when the Romans took over the area the folks that lived there already had a pantheon and festivals and all that stuff. They supposedly hadn't actually heard of JC or Mithras or the bunch before all this happened, or so most history books tell you. The thing is, the Celts had already been through Rome and Greece, and had done a pretty fair job of killing everyone there. In the midst of it, I figure they picked up some of the knowledge of these places amid the booty. The original meshing of religious myths probably started there, not in the fifth century AD, but we'll deal with what we know. The only real supposition I want to put forward in all this is the idea of the solstice being Roman. It doesn't affect anything, but I'm fairly sure the Romans and Greeks stole the idea from the Celts around 300 BC.

You see, Stonehenge, the Celtic rock pile that's stuck in some farmers' field in England to this day, was actually a solar calendar before it was a tourist trap. It measured the sun's movements, and marked all the solstices, etc. It also predates the Roman Solstice festivals by about 500 years. My guess is that it was the Celts that figured out the solstices and that the Greeks and Romans adopted the idea in the third century BC when the Celts were invading. What this means is that the festivals in Rome that led to the invention of Christmas were actually invented by a bunch of guys that not only weren't Christian, they weren't Roman or Greek either. Rome carried on the celebrations and adopted them into Christianity. Then, in the fifth century, they forced their version of it all on the Celts, who'd invented it in the first place. This is actually a pretty cool twist of fate in historical terms. Of course, I am also starkly aware that as a pick-up line in a bar this whole thing just doesn't cut it. It's kind of a "you had to be there" kind of thing.

The Celts had their own festivals which, over time, had drifted away from the Roman and Greek origins. Ideas of Jesus or Mithras or any of the Hellenistic gods didn't exist in the Celtic religion, but the festivals did. They'd developed their own ideas of what it was all about however, and it was these pagan Celtic additions to Saturnalia (now Christmas) that created some of the most beloved Christian traditions. (Oh..."Pagan"... It's a Latin word that keeps getting thrown around and misused, so I figure I should give a proper definition for it. Or as proper as I'm likely to get anyway. The modern word pagan comes from the Latin word Pagani. Note the addition of an "i" at the end. Use it. It makes you sound intelligent and adept, and you can easily intimidate people into thinking you're better informed than they are. Or so I've been told. Anyway, pagani is a blanket term that was used in Rome to describe any rural religion that didn't have an organized priesthood or temple. If it did have an organized temple or priesthood, it was religio, or religion without the "n". So... for rural religions you add an "i" to pagan. For urban religions you take the "n" off the word religion. Do this, and you will sound like you took three years of Latin in university. Trust me... that's about all you remember of 3 years of Latin after you've been out of university for a couple years...)

For those of you who actually got through all that, I'll now get back to trashing Christmas.

What all this amounts to is that the Celts and Norse interacted with the Romans and the Romans added stuff to Christmas that came from the Celts and the Norse. I know, I know... "Why the hell didn't I just say that to begin with?" Hey, if you're gonna tear down all the holy and sacred images these Xians put up every Christmas, you gotta have the facts behind you. Just looking at them and saying "This is stupid" doesn't work. Trust me on that one.

Here's a smattering of the things that came from the Celts and Norse...

Mistletoe

Oh what lies lurk in kisses! ~ Heinrich Heine

This stuff was originally used by the Druids (think of them as Celtic priests). Long before Rome Christianized the Celts, they believed that mistletoe was a powerful charm that warded off evil spirits, thunder, lightning, and all manner of ills. (Apparently it didn't work to keep the Xians away...) It also served as the

Celts answer to Viagra. Rumor had it that it could cure impotence and act as an aphrodisiac, so naturally it became popular in every Celtic household. I figure this was the real reason for its popularity among the Celts. The evil-spirit thing was just a cover story if you had friends over who saw Mistletoe hanging from your rafters. "Oh, THAT? Uh... yeah well, you see, the missus and me we're uh... being bothered by evil spirits. Yeah, that's it. Spirits. Nothing to do with impotence. Just plain old evil spirits. Nope...no impotence here. Ok, who's for another round of mead?"

The Roman missionaries looked at this whole aphrodisiac thing and thought "Hmmm...sounds like fun." So, of course, they banned it. Because of the sexual and pagan origin of the mistletoe myth, the plant was banned from the Roman Empire. It remained illegal right up the rise of the secular Christmas.

This aphrodisiac story is why you "have to" kiss someone who's standing under a twig of mistletoe. Originally it wasn't supposed to be a decision on your part. Supposedly any man and woman who met under it would both be caught under its spell. They would get so aroused that they'd take absolutely anyone who was close enough to grab. In this mad sexual frenzy, they would clutch each other and kiss passionately. In all likelihood, this tradition was actually just a cheap excuse to cop a feel in public.

There's also a Norse basis for the mistletoe thing. It has to do with Frigga, Odin's wife. The story goes that to protect Balder, her son, she made a charm that would guard against any injury from fire, water, air, or earth. But mistletoe wasn't really considered to be of fire, water, air or earth because it grows on trees as a parasite. Anyway, Loki, the evil god, had Balder killed with a dart made from mistletoe, and he goes to hell for three days. (Standard death sentence for divine beings apparently.) In the meantime Frigga swore that mistletoe would never again cause anyone any harm, so she supposedly kisses anyone who passes under it. The story is likely just a cleaned up version of the aphrodisiac story, but it's the accepted Norse version of mistletoe.

Caroling

Definition of Song: the licensed medium for bawling in public, things too silly or sacred to be uttered in ordinary speech. ~ Oliver Hereford

Ah yes... the hallowed Christmas tradition of turning your lights down low and locking the door so that the idiots coming down the street singing en masse think you're not home. I have so many warm Xmas memories of hosing down the sidewalk and watching from between drawn curtains to see how many flip. Not my memories of course. Personally I'd never do anything like that. But I've heard of people who do things like that. Read it in a book somewhere I think...

This whole tradition of Caroling is Celtic in origin. It's actually called Wassailing, but caroling is the modern English version of the same word. It means "to wish good health to a crop", usually apples or fruit. Supposedly the Celts would go door to door singing to bless the farmers for the next season of crops and wish them a bountiful harvest. In thanks the farmers would offer the wassailers a drink, usually mulled wine or hard cider or some other fruit alcohol beverage for the well-wishing. Then they'd all get tipsy and go off to the orchard where they'd blow horns and beat drums in an attempt to wake the tree from its winter slumber so it's ready for the upcoming spring. (Now, you KNOW that tradition started with some guy who was really pissed drunk and decided that singing wasn't enough, so he wandered out to the orchard to wake up the trees. There's always one in every crowd.)

There was actually an unstated community thing in all this too. You see, this was all done in the dead of winter when everyone was miserable and hating the weather. By going door to door, the crowd was able to check in on the elderly, sick, or just plain depressed folk to make sure they were still alive without having to make it look like they were being nosy. Even today we still wind up with the odd person who dies in December but no one finds the body until spring. The idea behind wassailing was to prevent that kind of thing. And get drunk for free from the farmers mead or cider.

Aside from the trying to wake up trees part, Wassailing wasn't inherently religious, so the Church just changed the songs sung to being Christmas songs and left the practice as it was. Nowadays people still carol, but they don't get as drunk doing it and, with the notable exception of Arkansas, nobody goes out and tries to wake up trees by singing to them.

Candles/Lights

What is true by lamplight is not always true by sunlight. ~Joseph Joubert

This is one of the Roman and Celtic overlaps. Rome had the idea of lights during their Saturnalia festivals. The Celts also had the same idea. There's nothing deep here. We're talking about traditions that happened in the middle of winter when the sun was at its weakest. Lights were kinda important.

The Celts had a festival around Christmas time called Candlemas. It eventually got bounced to February and is now what we in North America call Groundhog day, which is pretty far from the original celebration. It was a mid-winter house cleaning basically. You'd light a whole bunch of candles around the house and clean everything. The Celts had put a lot of mystic stuff into the lore of this candle mass idea... stuff about how you have to purge old stale energies. In reality it was a health thing. In the middle of winter things got pretty damned rank in small hovels. You needed a day set aside to get rid of the scum and soot and crap that would accumulate through European winters.

The Church allowed the idea of lighting tons of candles, eventually adopting them in to the Christmas idea as birthday candles for Jesus. This is the origin of the Christmas light. They were originally a Celtic ritual of cleansing, used in the dead of winter to revitalize the Celts home.

Feel free to emphasize this to your relatives. If it works, you'll be packing up the Xmas lights in about 20 minutes...

The Feast of St. Steven

Martyrs, my friend, have to choose between being forgotten, mocked, or used. As for being understood: never. ~ Albert Camus

You probably know that line from the carol "Good King Wenceslas last looked out on the Feast of Steven. When the snow lay round about, deep and crisp and even." The Steven they're talking about was a guy that Luke in the Bible made into a disciple after Jesus was dead and gone. The guy eventually pushed the Christianity thing to the wrong guys (namely the Sanhedrin, who were the local authorities in Jerusalem back then). The Sanhedrin got the Romans to beat the hell out of Steven, and they eventually threw him off a cliff and stood up top chucking rocks at him until he died. Hey... no one said religion was a nice thing.

Saul of Tarsus, who eventually became the apostle Paul, was a witness to this, and people say this was a factor in his decision to give up his career as a Christian killer and became a messenger from God. Oh well, we all make bad career choices. I, for instance, was once in the military.

Anyway, to celebrate this guy's bloody murder (sorry...martyrdom) the Catholics decided to hold a feast day. Not surprisingly, they put the feast on December 26 so it could fill in for some of the Roman Festivals. This way, the Christians could feel like it was ok to party with the rest of Rome.

While Steven's feast remained on the books, the feast itself never really took off until it got to Ireland. You see, after the priests explained this whole divine Jesus thing to the Celts, a lot of them were rather dubious of the concept. However, a celebration for a guy who was tossed off a cliff and stoned to death was something the Celts could relate to. So December 26 became a big day in Ireland as the Feast of Steven.

Good King Wenceslas

If you shoot at a king you must kill him. ~ Ralph Waldo Emerson

Wenceslas was born around 907AD. Because he was too young to rule, his mother, Drahomira, became regent. Drahomira was opposed to Christianity and openly opposed Rome. Wenceslas, unfortunately, put an end to the persecution of Catholic priests in Bohemia (present day Czechoslovakia) when he got old enough, so the Catholics like him. Accordingly, Catholic myth says he was nice to children, orphans and slaves. As Duke of Bohemia, Wenceslas' evil enemy was his brother, Boleslav. When Wenceslas's wife gave birth to a son, meaning that Boleslav was no longer his heir, Boleslav joined the nobles who were plotting his brother's assassination. He invited Wenceslas to a religious festival and then attacked him on his way to mass. While the two were "duking" it out, Boleslav's supporters jumped in and murdered Wenceslas. He died on September 20, 929 and is now the patron saint of the Czech Republic. Granted, that doesn't have anything to do with the Norse or Celts, but the St. Steven thing did, and I couldn't throw that in without adding the Wenceslas thing.

The Yule Log

This tradition was originally a whole bunch of logs, burned at Yule in honor of Thor, god of thunder and member of the Super Heroes Hall of Fame in Marvel Comics. I have no idea why burning a log was supposed to somehow specifically honor Thor, but apparently it did. Likely it had something to do with lightning (Thor's domain) starting forest fires.

It doesn't take a genius to figure out that lighting a fire log had something to do with the fact that it was winter. The eternal burning log represented the hope and light for the future during a cold, dark time of year. The Yule log, like a lot of the traditions, was adopted without question into Christianity, though the actual explanation for what it was doing there was lost to antiquity.

By adopting all this into Christmas (and Christianity in general) the Catholic Church attempted to quell the people of Ireland and Britannia, hoping to take over. By the 12th century the Church had killed or reformed the Celts and Norse, and it was deemed "Christianized". It was all kind of insidious, sneaking the Christianity into the Celtic festivals. The people barely noticed that over the course of a century their entire heritage had been overthrown, their myths corrupted, and their money flowing happily towards Rome.

But Rome was not in the habit of leaving things be. The popes knew that people left to their own would, sooner or later, start thinking on their own, and that was bad. So they left saints and bishops and priests to scare them into submiss...er, educate the masses.

As it turned out, however, this wasn't enough. The people still kept coming up with their own ideas. Ideas like "Hey, how come so much of my annual income has to go to Rome?" or "Why does the Pope need so much money to do Christian work?".

In standard Christian form, they indoctrinated the people with the idea of a powerful GOD that watched them day and night counting their sins, ready to toss them into eternal hellfire for disobeying the Church.

Then, to drive home this idea, they added in a new character to the Xian tale. A guardian of sorts... someone who knew the will of God, could watch you day and night, and who had no problem meting out punishments in the here and now. His retribution for sins would be immediate and painful, his power almost infinite. He had one, small fallibility though: He only showed up on Christmas Eve.

Santa Claus

Oh yeah... this is gonna be fun....

Odin was the Lord of the Yule. He was a big guy. Not fat, just BIG. He had this long beard and a dominant fatherly image. The Norse used to see him as the paternal figure in the pantheon... the one whose judgments were the final decision in any debate. Not unlike Zeus. Odin was seldom heard from in the Norse culture, but once a year during the Yule celebrations he'd deign to leave Valhalla in Asgard (his home) to visit humans if they were worthy that year. This was just too easy for Rome to take advantage of...

Somewhere in the fifth century, the Church condoned this new addition to the Christmas myth, who they originally called Father Christmas. He acted as the ultimate priest (whom you would also call Father) and was seen (as were the clergy) as punisher or gift giver, depending on how good you'd been. The advantage that Father Christmas had over the priests was that he was endowed with mythic powers and knew all. This myth nicely off-set the powers of the priests, who could occasionally be duped, thus allowing people to get away with things behind the Church's back. With Father Christmas, there was nowhere to hide. He knew all, and could punish with impunity.

Hold Nickar

In order to sell this idea to the Celts and Norse of the day, they dragged up a lot of their own mythos and tossed it in to this new Father Christmas character. The idea here was to make this new guardian of Christianity more marketable... not quite a god (because that would be too pagan) but close enough to being a god that the people would fear him, yet human enough for the people to believe that he could feasibly walk through the door at any minute.

His original look, that of a stern fatherly type (usually wearing a green crown of ivy, a symbol of his strong manhood) was an amalgamation of Odin, the top Norse god, the Greek sea god Poseidon, and a Teutonic god named Hold Nickar. (Teutonic is just a name for the original people in Germany... heavily Norse based.) They basically took all the strong fatherly gods and rolled them all into one Father Christmas.

St. Nicholas

By the sixth century, the name Father Christmas had been replaced by the name St. Nicholas. Your average Catholic would tell you this is because St. Nicholas was beatified (sainted) around that time and his celebrations were condoned by the Church and adopted into Catholic lore. The whole Father Christmas idea, they now contend, was just a silly mistake by some wacky Celts. Here's how it actually went down...

The new myth of the Father Christmas went over pretty well. So well in fact that it didn't stay just with the Celts and the Norse, but began to bleed out into the Church as a whole. Priests and parents both found the invention of this disciplinarian and gift giver just too easy. Suddenly Santa could be the bad guy, and the parents and priests could just waive the responsibility. Thus began the ancient tradition of scaring the hell out of your kids because Santa's coming, making them go to bed early and stay quiet. (More on that in a bit.) The Father Christmas lore worked even better than Santa does today, as his image is far less playful and way more imposing than the current Santa Claus. He was also about 12 feet tall, so you can imagine the idea of getting a beating from him for being bad would be a pretty scary concept.

Anyway, while all this was getting more popular in the fifth and sixth century, a couple things of note happened. Despite the Church's wishes, the name Father Christmas didn't catch on that well. People kept calling the new icon after the Teutonic name--Hold Nickar, or Nickar for short.

"No... that is NOT Hold Nickar!!! It's Father Christmas!!!" the priests would have to scream over and over.

"Oh. Well it sure LOOKS like Hold Nickar." the people would respond. "Is it his brother?"

At this point in the conversation the priests would normally just go screaming down the aisle, pulling their hair out in total frustration. The people, left to their own to figure it out, couldn't understand the resemblance. Totally unsure of what was going on in the ranks of the gods, the people took to just calling the image "Nickar", figuring they were covering all their bases that way. The Church, confronted with the popularization of the name Nickar, had to act quickly to include it in their mythos. Enter Nicholas of Myna, aka, St. Nicholas.

St. Nicholas of Myna; Patron Saint of Mariners

A little inaccuracy saves a ton of explanation. ~H. H. Munro

Now, there's some debate as to whether or the not the actual guy, Nick, really existed. But as the Catholics pretend that he did, we'll pretend that he did. So, the wool appropriately placed over our eyes, let's look at the life and times of Nicholas of Myna as dictated by the Catholics.

Around the time the Church was writing its new Bible (fourth century), there was a guy named Nick living in Myna, Turkey. Yes... that would be Turkey. Not the North Pole... Turkey. No workshop with vertically challenged peons making toys. No sleigh. The guy never saw a reindeer in his life. In all likelihood he wore only a brownish robe with a cheap rope to bind it with. No red suit, no bells, no black boots. He probably did have a long beard though... pretty typical for monks who had no interest in picking up women.

Nick lived a fairly average life for a monk in Turkey in the fourth century. The only real story we have about him has something to do with three virgins and a lot of money. Unfortunately, this story is nowhere near as interesting as its potential. Apparently, there was this father who had three daughters and no money. This meant he had no dowry he could use to bribe some guy into marrying them. (Back then you never got married unless the father of the bride gave you cash to pay for her upkeep. This practice carried through to the late Victorian era when men finally figured out that the women could actually have jobs and earn money too. Apparently we still haven't figured out that this also means they can pay for dinner and drinks.) Anyway, the father decided he should sell the daughters off into prostitution, since he wasn't going to get rid of them any other way.

Well, it seems old Nick had some cash lying around, so he chucked a bag of coins through the father's window one night. The father used this cash for a dowry for his first daughter and she got happily pawned off on some guy she probably didn't want to marry but had to. Seeing this, Nick tossed another bag o' cash through the window, and the same thing happened to the second daughter. On the third bag of cash, Nick got caught and the father thanked him profusely.

There's a famous picture of St. Nick with three bags of gold beneath him that supposedly represents this tale. The thing about it is, the picture got spread all through Europe after Nick became famous, and the tale that went with it got corrupted. You see, the way the picture is set up, you can't tell that it's three bags of gold. All you see is the tops of the bags at about waist level. The myth soon started that these three bags were actually children's heads. Then, as these stories go, a myth grew up about what Nick was doing with the heads of three children. Soon the story went that the three kids had been decapitated and that when St. Nick found out about the decapitation he went over and put the heads back on. The kids came back to life, thus proving St. Nick was actually a saint. (There's no mention as to whether Nick actually got the right heads on the right bodies. The implications here overwhelm my mind...)

When Nick died in 340 AD, the Church canonized him as the patron saint of mariners. Then, in the sixth century when the Church was confronted with the rise of the name Nickar for Father Christmas, they dug up the story of

Nicholas of Myna and put him forward as the true Father Christmas and the reason for the name Nickar. The masses heard all this, and basically thought "Oh... yeah... Nickar/ Nicholas. Now I've got it. I guess it wasn't Nickar after all." And so Father Christmas, now called St. Nicholas, was fully adopted into Christianity.

Santa Expands

The idol is the measure of the worshipper. ~ James Russell Lowell

Over the next few centuries this whole St. Nicholas myth became part and parcel of the Christian lore, with Nick and JC running neck and neck for Christmas popularity. No reindeer or flying sled yet, but Nick was still doing pretty good for himself. He'd become a powerful guy that would show up once a year to punish the bad and reward the good. Too bad he'd been dead for a couple of centuries at the time. I suspect he'd have liked the laurels.

The Church did develop this problem of Nickar, er, St. Nick being too much of a good guy. It seems the pagan beliefs they stole the image of St. Nick from all represented a kindly gift giver. The problem was that Rome was far more interested in keeping the people in line than with rewarding them when they were good. The punishing idea of St. Nick was what had to be stressed, not the kindly gift-giving. To facilitate this, all the local priests were told to tell the parents gruesome tales of the horrid things St. Nick did in the way of beating bad children, stealing bad children, and killing bad children. The parents, being uneducated and usually pretty naive, bought into these tales, passing them along as bedtime stories year round so that by Christmas the kids were too scared to think or move, let alone sin.

Sinter Klass

Man's mind is so formed that it is far more susceptible to falsehood than to truth. ~Desiderius Erasmus

An interesting thing happened in all this. By the 15th century the only hold out in Europe was Holland. While they eventually gave in to the December 25th date for the Hold Nickar/St. Nick festival (it had originally been on December 6), they still had a problem losing the Odin connection. You see, Holland was always more influenced by the Norse than the Celts, so the Norse myth of Odin is what they created the St. Nicholas idea out of. The priests dutifully explained who this Nick guy was, but a lot of the Dutch never really caught on to the Christian side of it all. After a lot of fiery speeches by the

Catholic priests, the Dutch eventually got the idea that Nicholas was a Christian bishop of some kind, and that he came once a year. What they never did figure out was why he looked so much like Odin, who also came once a year.

What you wound up with in the end was another compromise. The Dutch adopted the name St. Nicholas but called him Saint Nikolass, which became Sinter Klass, Dutch for Saint Nick. It's from the Dutch tradition that we first start seeing a St. Nick that looks like the one we're used to seeing. You see, true to the Norse tradition of Odin, Sinter Klaas was able to fly. Since he was a mortal of sorts, the Church decided Nick shouldn't fly under his own powers as Odin had because it just seemed too god-like. So, they gave him a flying horse. This kept Sinter Klass as close to mortal as the Church could keep him, but maintained the basics of the Odin myth. He was also sometimes pictured as arriving by flying boat, carrying the Book of Life that St. Peter supposedly lent to him so he knew who was good or bad that year. Then, to further distinguish Sinter Klass from Odin, the Dutch Church donned him in a red bishop's robe that flowed to the ankle.

The red outfit (that of a bishop) became the popular image of St. Nick throughout Europe from that time onwards. There are a lot of mutations in the actual dress style of St. Nick over the years, but the color red, adopted from the bishop's robes, has always stuck with him.

Evil Santa

So let's catch up... by the 12th century or so what we end up with is this mish mash of Celtic, Christian, and Norse imageries thrown in to create a Christmas character named St. Nicholas, aka Sinter Klass. He was 12 feet tall, wore red robes, and traveled either by flying boat or flying horse, depending on who you were talking to. He also carried around St. Peters Book of Life that let him know who was good or bad.

Now, this might all sound kinda hokey or lame to you and me, but to the people of the day this was serious stuff. The Church was all the education they got back then, and they were taught from cradle to grave to believe in all this. Besides, these people had bought into a story of a god incarnate that walked on water, raised the dead, and gave his disciples the power to kill old people by merely talking to them (look it up... it's in Acts. Peter and Paul kill an old couple because they didn't tithe enough money). After all that, the idea of a giant guy in red robes flying in once a year seemed totally plausible.

Sacred Scare Tactics

We are punished by our sins, not for them. ~E. Hubbard

The Santa image became a pretty good scare tactic for the Catholic Church. That was actually St. Nick's main job... scaring kids into being good. Sure he was supposed to be bringing all the gifts too, but that side of it seemed to always take a back seat to the scaring the hell out of you part. When kids heard about him in Europe from about 800AD to 1500 AD, he was always this big, scary bishop character that would come and beat them to a pulp if they didn't do what the Church wanted. Even the parents were scared of this Saint Nick guy.

The really interesting part of all this (trust me, you're gonna want to read this one out loud to your Christian friends) is how the Church developed the bad-guy image from St. Nick. Nick of Myna was supposedly a pretty decent guy that would never go around beating people up or dragging small children out of bed to harm them. As this just didn't fit with the Catholic Church's ideas of what St. Nicholas should be all about, the holy and true church fathers sat down yet again to edit out a few more pesky facts from the true and holy Christian tale. What they found was that while they could de-emphasize the kindly nature of St. Nick, the story really needed something new if it was going to carry the deeply disturbing fearful tones they felt the St. Nick story needed.

To solve this dilemma, they stole a bunch of mythos from the one character in popular myth that they knew people would readily recognize and be scared stupid of: your friend and mine, The Devil.

Satan and St. Nick

As long as people believe in absurdities they will continue to commit atrocities. ~Voltaire

A lot of people think the names Satan and Santa are so similar that they have to have the same origin. I'd love to tell you you're right on that one, but, unfortunately, the two words are totally independent of each other. The word "Satan" is Hebrew, and originally meant "intellect" or "the will of man" (i.e. man's will as opposed to God's will). It later came to mean any enemy of God, or any "will" that opposes the divine plan. (I could point out here that my name is Will, but as I overused that joke in The Heathen's Guide to World Religions, I figure I should just carry on).

The name Santa is just a version of Saint, which comes from the Latin Sanctos or sacred. A lot of religions in Rome had the idea of the sacred and the profane, that is, the area that was affected by the god's presence (the sacred) and the area outside the divine influence, called the profane. A saint is merely a person whose being is supposedly effected by the actions or influence of a god, so he or she is considered "sanctos" or saintly. This is also where we get the idea of sanctuary... a place where the influence of a god grants a person safety.

Anyway, the two words are not the same. One's Hebrew and one's Latin. Before you get too disappointed though, you'll be happy to know that there are a lot of other tie-ins between St. Nicholas and the devil that should drive any good Christian to go ripping down Santa paraphernalia

This is where we start getting a lot of the modern ideas of Santa. You should pull out a pen and start jotting this stuff down for use in casual conversations with religious wackos over this Yuletide season. Ok... some input from Satan:

St. Nick/Old Nick

In many parts of Europe, Satan is known as Old Nick. Likely Old Nick was also a derivative of Holt Nickar, but this manifestation of the Teutonic god wound up personifying the evil Satan. The Church looked to the Old Nick character to borrow some of the most fearful aspects of the St. Nicholas character.

The Candy Cane

In the myths of Old Nick, he would carry a crooked cane, the origin of the candy cane. It was used to capture lost souls by hooking them with the crooked end of it and drawing them in.

The North Pole

Until the church overlapped the myths of St. Nick and Old Nick, St. Nick was always believed to sit up in Heaven until he came down at Christmas to beat the kids. This changed with the introduction of Old Nick myths into St. Nick lore. In Europe the devil is always described or envisioned as living "in the north." All that is good is south, all that is evil is north.

This probably originates from the Norse, who actually traveled the world and figured out that North is cold as hell, and South is warm and plentiful. Both ways, North was evil and that's where people placed Old Nick's residence. When the church adopted the myths, St. Nick moved from Heaven to the North Pole. This has to be the worst example of job relocation in history.

Flying Reindeer

Nick already had the flying horse or boat idea from the Norse, but when the church added in the Old Nick myths suddenly Nick's transport was downgraded from horse to reindeer. (This was definitely an exercise in downsizing.) You see, Old Nick flew as well, but did so by attacking some poor innocent animal and putting him under his spell.

The animal was then his beast of burden until it died of exhaustion from flying at top speeds around the world. In the Old Nick myth it could have been any animal, but the myths stuck with the idea of reindeer because they were plentiful up north where Old Nick, aka St. Nick, came from.

Milk and Cookies

The idea of leaving a "treat" out for Saint Nicholas was originally a bribe. In Eastern Europe people would leave out bits of expensive foods for Old Nick as a bribe so he wouldn't take their children away. It was thought that the bribe from the parents could forestall Old Nick's vengeance on a person who rightly deserved to be punished. The Christians adopted the idea of idea leaving a bribe, mainly to give the parents something to munch on while the kids were cowering in their bedrooms.

Christmas Gnome

Until the overlap of St. Nick and Old Nick, St. Nick had always been seen as being 12 feet tall, reminiscent of Odin. When the Church redesigned him to be more like Old Nick, they also adopted his physique. Old Nick was often depicted as an ugly gnome (an image obviously stolen from Scandinavian myth of the ugly trolls who lived underground and hated humans) with big eyes and clawed hands that could rip you to bits. Again you'll note that St. Nick was not doing well in all this.

Chimneys

Now that St. Nick wasn't 12 feet tall, he was seen as being able to sneak in to your house to steal your child. While you could bar the doors, windows, etc., the one open passage in any house back then was always the chimney, which had to be open to allow smoke out. Since the chimney couldn't be sealed, it was seen as the most vulnerable point of entry. The Church capitalized on this, telling people that no matter what they did St. Nick would find a way to enact his vengeance if the children weren't good.

This was not done to show how quaint or small St. Nick was (as may be thought nowadays) but to show how resolved and determined his vengeance would be. Chimneys were and are sooty, horrid places covered in creosote. No one in their right mind would willingly go down one, so having this Christmas character ready and willing to crawl through all the crap in the chimney to get to you was a pretty scary proposition. (I imagine St. Nick did NOT appreciate this addition to his job description.)

Santa's Magical Sack

The original idea of the "magic sack" was to carry the bad children away in. The magical property of Santa's sack was that it could carry as many children away to torment and damnation as he wanted to stuff in to it. This "sack" image may originate from the whole gold and virgins story, but by the time it was incorporated into the myth it had less to do with giving money and more to do with delivering evil children to the waiting claws of the demons of Hell.

Let's Not Forget The Baby Jesus

The idea of an innocent baby Jesus really worked well into this Santa story for the Catholic Church at the time. While St. Nick was the punisher, the baby Jesus was portrayed as the innocent victim of our sins (a theme that still comes up in conversations with Christians). The idea here was that Jesus didn't need to be born and suffer on earth because he was perfect, but did so because we slimy evil humans needed someone to take on all the punishments for our sins. Oddly enough, this theology led to an increase in the acceptability of punishments from the Church. The logic was that by assuming your own punishments (as freely meted out by the priests and bishops) you were taking the pain away from the sweet innocent baby Jesus. If you didn't take your punishments, they'd just be passed on to this infant and you'd have to live your whole life knowing that the baby Jesus would get whipped and beaten because of YOU.

So, when St. Nick (or the clergy) came calling to exact punishment on the sinners, it was either you or the baby Jesus that got it. As it was so obviously your fault (whatever it was) leaving the infant to take your punishment was seen as a slimy and evil trick on your part. Thus the idea of Jesus as the Ultimate Sacrifice became the means by which the Church got people to accept the very punishments that the Bible said Jesus took for you. This is all pretty weird I grant you, but it worked for the Church. The end result was a bunch of mindless sheep that would line up and allow their children and themselves to be punished in the name of the sweet, innocent baby Jesus.

The actual Christ Mass on December 25 became an annual reminder of the sweetness and the purity of the infant whom your sins were going to torture and condemn. It was pretty far removed from the joyous, warm celebration you see nowadays at midnight mass on Christmas eve. Back then (up to about 1500 AD) the Christ Mass was a horrid condemnation of humanity designed to stress the whipping, torture, and degradation the Christ Child was going to have to endure to atone for our transgressions. As these tortures are almost identical to a lot of my favorite sins, I'd be willing to go with that "Do unto others" concept on this one.

Come 1500 AD though, there was a major shift in the Santa image. St. Nick suddenly became a nice guy. Theologians tend to say that this happened because the church and the world in general realized that there was a loving aspect to God (and his servants, like St. Nick). Suddenly St. Nick (or Sinter Klass) was more about love and gifts than punishment. (As, I might add, was the image of Jesus at the time. He too suddenly went from being the Ultimate Judge to being the Ultimate Defense Lawyer for Humankind). Like I say, this was supposedly because the Church realized that there was a loving and kind aspect to the character of God. This, of course, is crap. In the fifteenth century the Church was running scared and they'd use anything, even loving kindness if it came to it, to maintain control.

Reformation Santa

Martin Luther was a Catholic priest in Germany in 1515. Schooled in all the myths of the Church, including the Sinter Klass/St. Nicholas myth, he looked at it all and flipped.

Now, granted the idea of a Catholic priest flipping out was probably not that uncommon an occurrence given what they were told to preach. The thing is though,

Luther actually managed to turn the political tide against the Catholics for the first time in a thousand years. Making a long story short, Luther rebelled against Rome because he saw the Church as greedy, self-serving, and cruel. (Where he got an idea like that is beyond me) He had a real problem with the Church taking so much money from everyone and blowing it on opulence while the parishioners were starving and miserable. He felt that the Church had failed to provide the kind of loving, Christian environment that he thought the Church should as God's representative on Earth. More importantly to our tale, Luther thought the idea of punishment needed to be de-emphasized in Christianity and that the loving nature of God should be emphasized. The carrot before the stick basically.

This whole thing led to what they call the Reformation. Martin Luther left the Catholic Church, narrowly escaped being killed by them, and then rounded up a lot of support from the monarchs of Europe who all sided with him on the idea of love and peace and Christian sharing. The fact that this meant the monarchs could declare autonomy from the Church on the grounds of Luther's revelations (and therefore not have to pay tithes to Rome or do as the Pope said) supposedly had little to do with the popularity of Luther's message of love. Yeah... right.

Anyway, what you wind up with in the 16th century is a Christianity that emphasized love instead of discipline, caring instead of Crusades. Rome was on the ropes. The rise of the Reformation had them scared. They killed as many of the opposition as they could, but still the movement grew. So, as they always had in the past when confronted with a new idea that threatened their hegemony, the Church decided to adopt it all. The Catholic theologians set to work, writing and re-writing their canon law, trying to insert as much of this new love stuff as they could so the people would stop rebelling and get back to paying their tithes.

Among the things that had to be edited was Sinter Klass, the cruel and unforgiving bishop that came once a year to punish the kids for being bad. Dusting off the old texts, they discovered that he was also supposed to be bringing presents. Confronted with the need for a loving and kind public image, the Catholic Church decided this gift giving aspect of Nicholas, the bishop of Myna, would come in handy.

Love and Christmas

Love is a serious mental disease. ~Plato

In the late 16th century and on into the 17th the Roman Catholic Church popularized the idea of Sinter Klass giving gifts to kids who have been good. This showed him as the kind of loving, decent, and just character that the people wanted to see. The Reformation guys, by then known as the Protestants (as in those who protested against Rome) looked at the new image of Sinter Klass and basically agreed that this kind of gift-giving guy was an acceptable image for their new churches to adopt, so Sinter Klass was adopted by the Protestants.

The problem was, there was still the beating the kids part of it all that didn't sit well with a lot of folks. Through the Renaissance and Enlightenment eras, the Church (and now all the Protestant sects that were popping up everywhere) all began emphasizing the loving, kindly nature of God. St. Nick, as God's representative on Earth, had to toe the line and become loving, kind, and giving. However, the Church and, presumably, the parents, didn't want to lose that whole "scaring the hell out of the kids" part of the Santa story because it worked too well. So, yet again the religious elite went back to the drawing board to come up with a new addition to the Santa myth: Black Pete.

Black Pete

Bigotry murders religion to frighten fools with her ghost. ~ Charles Caleb Colton

If you're from North America you've probably never heard of Black Pete. He's a part of the Christmas story that was entirely lost when it crossed the Atlantic. But in Europe, especially in countries like Poland, Germany, and Holland, the character Black Pete remains a staple in Christmas lore. Pete was a young, black boy who traveled with St. Nick on his annual rounds. He's often depicted with a twisted, evil leer on his face, carrying a riding crop or cane. He's about 4 foot tall, and is shown either naked or dressed in rags. This character, Black Pete, became the Punisher; the one who exacted the divine retribution on the children thus leaving St. Nick's hands bloodless and pure. It was Black Pete that did the evil (but necessary) spanking, beating, and hauling off to eternal damnation. St. Nick, as God's messenger on Earth, was free of the guilt of ever having to hurt anyone.

Now, I could go on about the obvious racial slurs involved in the creation of this character, but I figure the anti-black imagery is so blatantly obvious in this that I needn't lend any credence to it by emphasizing it. Suffice to say that the white-bred religious leaders of the day invented this character to epitomize all that was scary and evil in the world. To the Europeans of the day the image of a black boy was something exotic and wild; totally divorced and uncontrolled by their elite white society. (Again, this is crap, I know. I get worried when I write about stuff like this that there are people out there that are going to figure I'm agreeing with this kind of idiocy merely because I report on it.)

Anyway, Pete became the instrument of God's retribution throughout Europe. The children were told that St. Nick was coming, but that Black Pete would be with him. If they were good, St. Nick would leave presents and candy for them. If they were bad, Black Pete would come to their rooms in the night and beat them or drag them away to eternal damnation. Thus Christmas Day became a mini Judgment Day, with St. Nick playing the role of Christ and Black Pete being Satan.

Nowadays you seldom see Black Pete stuff anywhere, mainly because the North American marketing of Christmas has all but forgotten the character. But if you happen to find yourself in Romania or some such place, you're likely to find yourself listening to one of the elders telling spooky tales about Black Pete, scaring the hell out of the kids before they go to bed on Christmas Eve.

Oliver Cromwell

Cromwell was the whip for the Puritan movement in England. These guys are in my top 10 "Who To Hate in History" list. Basically, the Puritan's decided (for some stupid reason) that England and all of its colonies should actually be run on 'true' Christian principles. This meant intolerance, prudence, abstinence, sobriety, and a whole bunch of other things that they would have hated me for.

It was Cromwell and his Cronies who figured out that Christmas really had absolutely nothing to do with Christianity. It seems a couple of them actually took the time to read up on the Saturnalia festivals and the whole Odin connection and thought, "Wait a minute... this has absolutely nothing to do with Christianity!" (a revelation that has yet to occur to most contemporary Christians.) To this end, the Cromwell Cronies nixed the idea of Christmas in England in the 17th century. Basically, from 1630 until about 1830, Christmas was non-existent in popular English culture. Why? Because it was evil, evil, evil! (Kinda brings a tear to my eye...)

We'll be going into much greater detail on these nut-bar Puritan guys in a short bit, but understand that they managed to kill the idea of Christmas in

England for about two centuries. St. Nicholas packed up his red sack, hopped on his reindeer, and meandered back to the North Pole in semi-retirement. Christmas, for all intents and purposes, was dead as a national holiday in this era. Unfortunately, like all popular religious phenomena throughout history, it just didn't have the God-given decency to stay dead.

A Christmas Carol

In 1843, Charles Dickens wrote and published A Christmas Carol. Little did he know at the time the hours of cruel torture he was inflicting on the masses by way of cheesy, black and white reruns and equally bad remakes. For instance, I'm fairly sure that this festive time of year, at least one of your relatives has tried to inflict on you the Christmas epiphany of one Ebenezer Scrooge as portrayed by one Alistair Simm. I am equally sure that you, like myself, have run screaming from the room only to be found hours later quivering beneath your bed sheets muttering something akin to "Not again... Can't they find ANYTHING else to broadcast in December?"

Well, thankfully they have. We now have An American Christmas Carol, The Muppets Christmas Carol, Mickey's Christmas Carol, and, my personal favorite, Scrooged with Bill Murray. Yes, now we have version upon version of this sappy, antiquated, morality play to sate the appetite of even the most masochistic Christian. Let me tell you how all this came into being...

The original story was published in a series of articles in London in 1843. It's basically the tale of the brainwashing of a perfectly reasonable and respectable businessman in 19th century Victorian England. The guy, Ebenezer Scrooge, starts out wealthy and successful and ends up literally tossing his money out the window in a vain hope to "redeem" his evil ways. Now, most people figure that the redemption in question is one from miserly and insensitive to caring and loving. Were this true, the story would have disappeared years ago without so much as a single reprint.

This story is what I consider the dawn of the Corporate Christmas. Its message? Spend money on other people and you will go to heaven. Don't and you will die a lonely, miserable death and go to hell. This is why it keeps coming back every year. Sure, people will tell you that it's because it's such a warm and loving story filled with hope and character. Well, so is Old Yeller, and you don't see remake after remake of that one.

A Christmas Carol is the first, clear message from the corporate merchants to the populace: SPEND. So subtly was this message put forward in Dickens' tale that even today people watch the various incarnations of it unaware of its true agenda. This tale, both as a book and as a movie, leaves the audience with a sense of hope, love, comfort, and joy manifest in the 'spirit' of Wal-Mart, Bi-Way, Zeller's, Costco, Gap, K-Mart, and, of course, Family. For what good are all these presents without people to give them to?

The family is the vehicle.

Using pathetic and cheap gimmickry, say, like a crippled, sweet, little boy, Dickens emotionally blackmails the audience. Literally stating, "this little boy is going to die a horrible, agonizing death if you don't spend your hard-earned money on him."

The proliferation of this story in no small way contributed to the resurrection of Christmas in the post-industrial era. The merchants now had a surplus of products they had to sell. They backed the books, the plays, the articles and, eventually, the movies spawned by Dickens' tale because they knew the message contained within it. Once again, Santa and all things 'Christmassy' were called out of retirement. Not for religious or political control, but to meet the new rising global challenge; economic prosperity.

An Old Fashioned Christmas

It's never safe to be nostalgic about something until you're absolutely certain there's no chance of its coming back. ~Bill Vaughn

Question: What is an "Old Fashioned Christmas?"

This kinda gets to me. I mean, every year you see these cards with candles and wreaths and gothic images of an "Old Fashioned Christmas" and everybody sits around and agrees that Christmas is not what it used to be. My question is, when exactly do they figure Christmas was what they portray it to be in these cards? The truth is, it never was like that. Let me show you what I mean...

All the pictures you see of the classic, warm, loving family Christmases are generally portrayed as occurring in about 1800. Horse driven sleighs, candles for lights, and heavy snow falls with children out playing happily. Unfortunately for the Hallmark people who make these cards, this picturesque image of Christmas just never happened. You see, Christmas didn't exist as a holiday in the United States until the late 1800's. Prior to this, the practice of Christmas was either irrelevant to the new settlers or outright illegal. In New England, for instance, businesses demanded their labor force to be in to work at 5 am on December 25 so that the workers wouldn't have a chance to go to church. If you missed school that day you were summarily expelled. To fully explain this phenomena, it is important to examine the Puritan culture and their effect on the legal and social history of the United States. Fortunately for both of us, however, I have absolutely no interest in fully explaining anything so I'll just shoot a couple random facts at you that'll give you the gist of the era we're talking about. I mean, who actually gives a damn about the Puritans anyway?

The Puritans in America

The Christian Right is neither. ~ Unknown

In 1712, the Rev. Cotton Mather of Boston wrote: ``The Feast of Christ's Nativity is spent Reveling, Dicing, Carding, Masking, and in all Licentious Liberty... by Mad Mirth, by long Eating, by hard Drinking, by lewd Gaming, by rude Reveling. Men dishonor Christ more in the twelve days of Christmas, than in all the twelve months besides.'' This was the early American sentiment towards Christmas.

You see, the Pilgrims that everybody talks about at Thanksgiving were Puritans. These are the same guys that killed young women in Salem for being witches. (Nowadays we put them on Oprah... I'm not sure which is worse). These guys are where we get the word Puritanical from. They're the absolutely fanatical, Hellfire and brimstone, we're-all-going-to-hell type Christian lunatic that makes this job of mine worth doing. They were one of the first groups to come to the Americas because they thought the Europeans were all hell bound, and they wanted to create a new world over here that was based entirely on their strict, bible-thumping views. Happily they've failed miserably, but their idea was originally to make the US into some kind of Ultra-Christian state where everyone abided by the strictest interpretation of the Bible they could possibly come up with. No dancing, no secular music, no swearing, that of sort of thing.

These Puritans wrote a lot of the original laws that governed North America. Not the Pledge of Allegiance, but also a lot of the codes and laws of the land. This, by the way, also explains why so many of the laws in the States are more stringent than their European counterparts where sex and morality are concerned; the Puritans wanted a land that was entirely pure and lust free. Since they believed everything fun was a cardinal sin, they passed laws accordingly. In particular, they hated things like dancing, drinking, and sex, so strict laws were enforced to make sure the early Americans had absolutely no fun.

When they got around to addressing the idea of Christmas there was no question about it; it was evil. Any kind of fun celebration that might bring about gifts or earthly pleasures was strictly forbidden, and they passed laws against it. As a result, celebrating at Christmas was an illegal practice in the New England states in the 17th century, most notably Massachusetts. Strict religious observances were ok, providing you didn't enjoy them. Laws were passed (before confederation) that made Christmas illegal in these states. Later, as the nation grew and states like Kentucky and eventually California came into being, the idea of Christmas became a non-issue. It was illegal in New England, so most of the other states just kind of shrugged and didn't bother with it. No state recognized Christmas as a holiday through to the 1800's. It just wasn't a big thing in the Americas. Individual immigrant families might recognize the holiday in their own homes, but it wasn't really that important. It had all the religious importance of, say, Shrove Tuesday (the beginning of Catholic Lent). Some people adhered to it, but for the most part it was just a "religious" thing that the new world wasn't concerned with.

As a result, Santa and a lot of the myths of Christmas just didn't carry over to the New World. From 1630 to about 1830 Christmas didn't effectively exist in America. Then came the Irish.

The Potato Famine

A prohibitionist is the sort of man one couldn't care to drink with, even if he drank. ~Henry Louis Mencken

On September 9, 1845, the first news story appeared in the Irish papers alluding to a crop failure in the potato industry. From there on in, it all turned to hell. Potatoes were the main food for the country, and when they dried up there was literally no food for most of the nation. Trust me, this does actually get around to being about Christmas. I promise.

You see, a whole heap of these Irish folks got together and, figuring that there was no food in Ireland, they hopped boats for Canada and the United States. The early 1800's saw a huge influx of Irish immigrants into the States, which meant a huge influx of Irish and Celtic culture coming in as well.

We owe far more to these poor, starving immigrants than any of us usually stop and consider. While the Dutch, Spanish, Germans and English had established the roads and cities of North America, the Irish brought with them a cultural icon that would forever alter the face of North America in ways no historian will ever be able to fully credit: The Irish Whisky.

You see, a lot of these Irish folks settled in to New England (Boston in particular). This area, you'll recall, was the same area that had been founded and settled by the Puritans. By the 1800's a lot of their puritanical views had kind of waned and a secularism was starting to thrive, but there were still a lot of laws and folkways that reflected the Puritans ideals. Most forms of carnal fun were frowned upon in Bostonian culture back then. It was all very prim and proper. Then along came the Irish, and with them the introduction of Irish Whiskey; the single most powerful cultural influence these uptight Bostonians had seen since the Civil War. The Irish basically waded in to this new culture, looked at the uptight, puritan lifestyle these New Englanders were living, then laughed like hell.

What the Irish brought was a sense of fun. They'd come out of a famine, and because of this they'd learned to work hard and prosper. But at the same time they knew that life had to be lived rather than endured. So, they worked hard and they partied hard. Irish pubs started appearing all over New England, with loud raucous get-togethers happening pretty much every night. The Irish Whiskey was flowing, and the tide of it swept through the entire New England culture. The stoic, old school puritanical views quickly gave way to a new, carpe diem attitude that the Irish had brought with them. Partying, real partying, was suddenly socially condoned and encouraged. By 1870 New England was totally transformed from stodgy and uptight to free, happy, and ready to enjoy life to the fullest. I credit this era as the turning point American legal ethics. It's the demise of the puritanical Christian state and the rise of independent, "live and let live" ethics.

So it was that the Irish moved in and changed the face of the east coast of the US forever. Gone were the days of harsh and inflicted Christian purity and chastity. With the addition of the Irish and their whiskey, drunken revelry, parties, and being a member of the Kennedy family became acceptable and encouraged social behavior.

The Irish and Christmas

I have to point out here why these New England states are so important to this story. You see, at the time most of the US was still trying to get its shit together. Places that are now major cities were still struggling to keep the bears off the main streets. Sewage was a pipe dream. Homes, in most of the territories, were still little more than shacks with chickens running through them.

But places like Boston and Philadelphia were well established. As they didn't have to worry about things like mountain lions eating their children, they had the spare time to start worrying about things like the Constitutional amendments. So it was that what happened in New England at this time was reflected in the laws of the nation.

A lot of folks will tell you that the Irish brought the myth of Christmas over to the United States when they arrived with the famine. That's basically true, but you gotta understand that other European cultures brought their ideas of Christmas with them (i.e.: the Dutch, Polish, etc.) but they didn't manage to fundamentally change the way Christmas was celebrated in the US. The Irish did. Here's how...

First off, there were a lot of them. When a Dutchman moved into New England at this time he'd be assimilated. That is, he'd have to abide by the rules and laws that were set down by the Puritans a couple centuries earlier. The Irish managed to move in en masse, and just take over a lot of the areas, setting up their own rules. While they didn't immediately get rid of a lot of the idiotic laws about proper behavior, they did the next best thing by taking over the police forces such that the average cop on the beat was Irish back then. This meant that someone staggering out of a bar at 3 in the morning wouldn't wind up in jail for public indecency as would have happened before the Irish invasion. He'd just get sent on home by the Irish cop.

As time went by, the Irish filled a lot of positions in the society, including mayors, council men and, eventually, senators and congressman. Sure, the Puritanical views fought back, but the Irish sentiment (which opened a floodgate of similar sentiments around the US) really was the death of Puritanical Christianity in North America. The last battle in this cultural war was the 1920's prohibition movement that made alcohol illegal. The law stayed in place for a couple years and was struck down when...when... um. Damn. This is actually a really cool story, explaining how the Puritans were finally put in their place in North America and made to look like fools. The problem is I'm supposed to be writing about Christmas here, and as I haven't really tied it in the last couple pages I can't go off on the prohibition tangent I wanted to go on. Damn editors... they never let me have any fun.

The Irish are credited with reforming the puritanical laws of the early settlers of the United States. Other groups, most notably the Texans, worked to get the Church out of politics in the states (thank you, Texas). What you wind up with here is a growing sense of secularism, and a division of Church and State. Now, since the "Church" referred to in most early American literature is usually the Puritanical version, this meant that people were able to start deciding for themselves what they wanted to do about holidays. So it was that in the 1800's the idea of Christmas was able to start bleeding into American culture for the first time.

The American Christmas we all know and hate really started in this era. Now that you've got a handle on the social reforms that were going on at the time with the demise of the Puritan culture, I figure I should show you how all the Christmas myths and fantasies that we covered earlier finally found a home on American soil.

The Making of the Modern Christmas

Better to be known as a sinner than a hypocrite. ~Proverb

Ok... here's what we wind up with by 1830 or so;

There had been a lot of Christmas myths over the years throughout Europe, mostly because the churches could use the Santa story as a good scare tactic. To this day Christmas Mass remains the single biggest extortion (sorry... donation) day of the year. The need to go to church on Christmas was solidly ingrained in European culture as one of many guilt-ridden controls the religions used to keep the people in line. Throughout the Americas, however, the idea of Christmas was almost non-existent because the country had been founded by nut-bar Puritans who hated the idea of anything that might possibly be fun.

By 1830, however, the Puritans ideas were pretty much dead, and various groups in the states were starting to go back to their European heritage and were celebrating Christmas in their own homes. It was considered a minor holiday back then. No day off, no mass marketing. Just a day to remember that Jesus had been born and we should all feel guilty for it. Culturally though, the Irish immigrants had revamped the New England pompousness into a freer thought, and the States was ready to accept any new reason to party.

The weird part of all this is that no one was looking at Christmas to be that reason. Nobody pushed the idea on the people. No church stepped forward to inflict the Christmas celebration on the states. The Christmas myth hit the US in the early 1800's much the same way the Hula Hoop or the Beatles would hit later on: it was a fad, introduced to the US culture by way of a simple poem written by a miserable, bigoted theologian to keep his daughter out of his hair. Amazing how these things happen.

Clement Clarke Moore

Moore was a Hebrew scholar and the son of an Episcopal bishop, so you can figure we're gonna have problems with this guy right from the get go. He was born in Newton, Long Island in 1779. Being the kindly, religious guy he was he spent his life actively opposing things like democracy, the abolition of slavery, the vote for women, etc.. From all accounts the guy was a sour, curmudgeonly bastard that hated the whole planet. About the only thing he did seem to actually give a damn about was his daughter, and it was out of his fondness for her (or to shut her up, we're not sure which) that he sat down and wrote a poem based on the Christmas myths he'd learned in Bible school. At the time the tale of Sinter Klass and the whole reindeer idea had all but faded from American myth, having been relegated to the realm of theologians and historians like Moore. But Moore saw the chance to entertain his daughter with this ancient story about flying reindeer, so he wrote it out and handed it to her. If the poem had remained in her hands, Christmas would probably never have been big in the States and I wouldn't be writing this book. One kid, one story. No problem. But that ain't the way it happened.

You see, what Moore created in this poem was a mesh of the Dutch Sinter Klass we talked about earlier and the English St. Nicholas, a small, gnome-like Santa. What he came up with the very first image of the American Santa Claus.

He called his poem "A Visit From St. Nicholas"... the poem we all know and are tortured by every year under the name "Twas the Night Before Christmas." He wrote the entire poem in about an hour, scribbling it on a piece of paper while riding in the back of a carriage next to his daughter. He handed the page to her to read thinking it would keep her happy for a bit, then forgot about it.

Awhile later his daughter showed the poem to a cousin named Sarah Butler, who copied it into her diary. In 1823 Sarah's father read it while peeking through the diary, liked it, and sent it off to a newspaper in Troy, N.Y. The newspaper printed it and soon clippings of the poem were being seen everywhere. Suddenly the whole of New England knew and loved this St. Nicholas character. After this initial success, the poem made its way to New York and, eventually, L.A. and all points in between. The whole country became fascinated with this St. Nicholas character that Moore had written about. Thus began the rise of the Christmas tale in the United States. Not with Jesus or the Church or any of the religious dogma that had been Christmas in times before. The popular American Christmas rose almost entirely out of the popularity of this one poem, which in time spawned dozens of other stories, books, cards, and articles designed to capitalize on the stunning success of Moore's tale.

As an academic, Moore was embarrassed by the poem and didn't admit he wrote it until about 15 years later, when a book-length edition was printed. I suspect he finally had to set aside his academic pride for literary rights and percentages. I know I do.

The Rise of the American Santa

"People don't ask for facts in making up their minds. They would rather have one good, soul-satisfying emotion than a dozen facts." ~Robert Keith Leavitt

This is the real beginning of the Christmas concept as you and I know it in North America. Pretty much everything you've ever seen as being a part of Christmas was dragged up and introduced into American culture during this era. You see, the media went kinda nuts trying to keep up with this American Christmas fad. Amid the barrage of Christmas stories appearing in every magazine and newspaper, the merchants realized that what could sell newspapers could also be used to sell merchandise. It worked like this...

Through the late 1800's as this whole Christmas fad was running rampant, one of the basic Christmas ideas (mentioned in Moore's poem) was the idea of St. Nicholas bringing gifts. Now, you and I know that this story actually comes from the Norse idea of Hold Nickar and the gifts he brought with him. But Moore presented the white-washed, Christian version of it all with St. Nicholas showing up with presents for the good little boys and girls. Because he seemed to actually care about his daughter, Moore omitted the role of Black

Pete, the punisher, and just talked about the friendly gift-giving St. Nicholas. As no one really cared to look into the tale, the newspapers and merchants were happy to leave behind Black Pete the Punisher and just stick with the happy gnome. So, amid this new fascination with all things Christmassy, the idea of Americans giving gifts to each other at Christmas was proliferated. Through the late 1800's the gifts were usually just handmade toys and such; small trinkets designed to reflect the quaint Christmas custom that anyone who was anyone was adopting. You see, it just wasn't couth not to be into Christmas back then. It was haute cuisine.

Like I said, though, this was a fad. It wasn't based on religion or deep emotional ties to history or tradition. It was just something that cropped up in popular American culture because of one silly little poem that became extremely popular. In all likelihood the entire idea would have faded away as quick as the Hula Hoop if it weren't for the fact that the idea of giving gifts happened to work well into the budding American corporate culture. Put bluntly, Christmas survived because big business realized that this fad could be used to sell products in December, a month that was traditionally a poor sales month.

Faced with those cold, moneyless winter nights, the fledgling corporate America called on old Nick to save their butts come the

Christmas season. At approximately 1500 years of age, Nick wasn't exactly up to the task. But the marketing guys offered him a new suit, a couple more reindeer, and a bunch of elven slave laborers to sweeten the deal. When they threw in the wife, Mrs. Claus, the Bishop of Myna, Turkey, Patron Saint of Mariners (who had been celibate for over a millennium) took the job.

Saint Nicholas had been introduced to America, and the people loved him. Stories abounded about this cute little elf character that would sneak in and leave presents once a year, if you were good. The parents quickly learned that this could be used to torture the kids, so even with the loss of Black Pete the threat of not getting gifts soon paired with the promise of them. The horrors of Black Pete's divine retribution became "If you're not good, St. Nicholas will leave coal in your stocking." Hey, at least the kids weren't living in mortal terror anymore.

The name St. Nicholas soon got shortened to St. Nick, just because it sounded friendlier and easier to say. In about 1910 the name Santa Claus became popular, mainly because it was different and the old St. Nick name had gotten a little stale in marketing terms. "Santa

Claus" was just a bastardization of Sinter Klass, the Dutch name for St. Nick.

Now, the myth has it that the jolly Santa Claus figure in a red and white suit came from an artist named Haddon Sundblom who worked for Coca-Cola in 1931. This is kinda true. You see, the idea of St. Nicholas wearing a red suit goes way, way back to the time when they first canonized Nicholas of Myna. He was depicted as having the long flowing red robes of a bishop, which is what the guy was. The thing is, when Nick moved from Heaven down to the North Pole in the 1600's, they had to give him heavier clothes for those cold arctic nights (this was before Mrs. Claus was invented).

Anyway, he had been dressing in old, heavy furs since about the 16th century. He'd maintained that look through all the years when Christmas as a holiday was kinda being forgotten. In 1823, for instance, a New York printer named William Gilley (hoping to capitalize on the success of Twas the Night Before Christmas) wrote a poem about a "Santa Claus" who dressed all in fur and drove a sleigh pulled by one reindeer.

Haddon Sundblom, the guy that worked for Coke, just combined a lot of the existing elements of Santa Claus lore into a new, cleaned up version of St. Nick. Of course, the red used in Santa's outfit was, coincidentally, the exact same tint and shade of red used by Coke, so the Coca Cola PR team loved it. I might add here that the Pepsi team did not, and indeed tried to portray St. Nick in Green and white to combat the image. But they failed, and even Pepsi uses the standard red and white Santa Claus these days.

So it was the Coca Cola Santa, first drawn by Sundblom that became the standard of all Santas to this day. Gone were the rags and heavy furs that Moore's Santa had. Now, Santa had a proper red suit with white trim and black boots.

Kris Kringle

"One of the problems we have in this country is that too many adults believe in Santa Claus, and too many children don't"
Lee Lauer

I figure I should explain this whole Kris Kringle thing, since it still seems to pop up in the odd Christmas cartoon.

While all these Santa developments were going on in the US, Germany was busy working out its own St. Nicholas image. They had the Hold Nickar type Santa; the gift-giver/divine retribution guy. But this image got kinda tossed aside by the Methodists and Lutherans in the 1800's. They had this whole religious revolution in Germany at that time that tried to place the focus of Christmas onto the infant Jesus (no idea where they'd get a silly idea like that, but that's what they tried for anyway). Hold Nickar/St. Nicholas was replaced for a short time by the baby Jesus (the Christ child, or "Christkinderlein"). Since the St. Nick lore was so deeply entrenched they found they couldn't toss him out altogether, so they had the Christ Child travel around with a mysterious parent figure (a throw-back to the Norse "Father Christmas" idea of the 4th century. This is what became Pere-Noel in France).

Anyway, this parent figure would visit kids while they were still awake and scare the hell out of them. The next morning when the kids woke up (if they could actually get to sleep after being tormented in their beds the night before) they'd find gifts lying around. The story had it that while the Pere Noel was scaring them, the Christ Child, or Christkinderlein, had left the gifts.

Over time this whole Christkinderlein idea just kind of flopped, and everyone gave up trying to pretend that the Christ Child had anything to do with Christmas. The St. Nicholas myth came back full force in Germany by the late 1800's and everyone just kind of forgot about the whole attempt at a Christian Christmas.

The legacy of all this is that the German name for the Christ Child, Christkinderlein, got Anglicized to "Kris Kringle" and was adopted into the Santa myth when they gave up trying to involve the baby Jesus in the whole mess. So it was that Kris Kringle became one of the names of Santa Claus.

Mass Marketing Santa

In general, my children refused to eat anything that hadn't danced on TV. ~Erma Bombeck

Now, you'll notice that there's less and less mention of the religious side of this Christmas thing. That's kind of the point. There's never really been a religious (or at least Christian) mandate to the existence of Christmas. The fact that Christmas ever had anything to do with the late great JC was entirely a concoction of the Christians in the fourth century. In this era, as the Christmas holiday took North America by storm, there really was no concern for the religious premise of the holiday. It just didn't matter. Those that really pushed for Christmas to become an integral part of North American culture (marketing guys mainly) were happy to hear that the religious right could accept the holiday as part of their culture, but the reality is that Santa would have sufficed. What they did need was Santa Claus; the perfect gift-giver.

One of the things that worked really well in all this was Santas reputation for knowing "who's been naughty and who's been nice." Originally (before Moore) St. Nicholas knew who was good or bad because he traditionally had access to St. Peter's Book of Life. With this new Santa image, the North American Santa just sort of "knew" things because he was magic. Granted, a Christian could see this and think it was a divine gift, but no divine contact was ever stressed with the North American Santa. His job was sales, and that's why Moore's Santa became popular. Because he "knew" things he was presented as being able to "know" in some magical way what gift would be perfect for the friend or relative you didn't know how to buy for. This kind of magic was exactly what the marketing people were looking for. Santa Claus, as the representative of Christmas in America, has appeared on TV, radio, and print to sell everything from soda pop to cars to lawn furniture. To my knowledge, the baby Jesus has yet to do even a single Pampers commercial.

Santa Supreme

The dominion of Santa over the Christmas holiday was firmly entrenched after a much publicized letter to Francis Church, Editor of the New York Sun. This is the famous "Yes, Virginia, there is a Santa Claus" letter. I gotta cover this basic story not because I have any use for the warm, loving sentiment of it but because it poignantly demonstrates the shift from the Christ child to Santa Claus as the focal point of Christmas in America. The story is sappy but it goes like this:

The New York Sun's motto was "If you see it in the Sun it's so." This was a credo that the Sun's staff lived by. The newspaper had a reputation for only printing 'the truth'. So, when a young girl named Virginia wrote a letter to the Editor asking if Santa Claus really existed, it was incumbent on the Editor to only answer truthfully. The girl had stated that if no response was given then she would automatically accept that as a 'no'. Here the Editor was put into the awkward position of having to tell a little girl that no Santa Claus existed. In a much publicized response Francis Church established the existence of Santa Claus with the following words,

"He exists as surely as love and generosity and devotion exists, and you know that they abound and give to our life its highest beauty and joy. Alas! How dreary would the world be if there were no Santa Claus! It would be as dreary as if there were no Virginia's. There would be no child-like faith then, no romance, no poetry to make tolerable this existence.

We should have no enjoyment except in sense and sight. Yes, Virginia, there is a Santa Claus!" (The New York Sun "Is there really a Santa Claus?" December 10, 1897).

This letter was written in 1897, but has been reprinted liberally ever since. You'll note that amid all this sentiment, you will NOT find the name Jesus, or any mention of Christian ethics. This letter marks the emancipation of Santa Claus from Christian myth. He becomes the embodiment of all of the virtues that Christianity used to place on Christ. Just as the Jesus myth was derived from the Pagans, this was the dawn of a new pseudo-religious figure independent of the Judeo-Christian window dressing. From here on in, Santa was on his own.

Leaving Jesus Behind

The McCarthy Era brought back a bit of the puritanical Christian right. They're kind of like that one weird relative that everyone hates but you have to invite to reunions. As soon as you let them in the door they suddenly try to take over everything and eventually you have to just chuck them out the door. That scenario pretty much sums up what happened in the 50's, and why there was such a revolution in the sixties. During the McCarthy era there was a pretty good attempt on the part of the right wing Christian communities to wrest control of the Christmas season from the secular, fairy tale Santa Claus image that was growing.

For a while Santa and the baby Jesus vied for the people's favor during the 50's, but in the end it was no contest. Basically, the baby Jesus supporters maintained that His name was actually on the holiday and that by virtue of that the holiday should be His. Santa, as the duly appointed spokesman for Corporate America, maintained that although Jesus' name might be part of the word "Christmas", it was Santas happy, non-Christian gift-giving that was responsible for approximately 20% of the Gross National Product for the

United States. The baby Jesus really didn't have much of a retort to that one.

When the social and political revolution took hold in the sixties, the marketing people who were using Santa Claus realized that the topic of religion (Christianity in particular) had become absolutely taboo. While they wanted and needed to maintain the holiday (and the revenues that went with it) they had to drop any residual Christian overtones that went with Santa, Christmas, and gift giving. It was in this era that the last vestiges of a Christian pretense were dropped from the Christmas season. The marketing boards started digging up every non-Christian Santa myth that could be found or invented. So too did the movie makers, television writers, and McDonald's head office. (i.e.: you WILL see Santa in a McDonald's commercial. You will NOT see a baby Jesus.)

The Magic of Christmas

The word 'magic' actually comes from the Persian word 'Magi' meaning 'enchanted'. This was a form of oral incantation; basically, you said something in the right way and it happened. (You'll note this is also the name of the Three Wise Men.. the "Magi." They supposedly practiced this kind of mystical art.) Anyway, somewhere along the line Santa Claus became magical. (I don't know... maybe he found a book somewhere or something. You have a lot of time to read up in the North Pole in June). This was likely a throwback to the Norse myths; you'll recall that Odin was one of the figures adopted into the St. Nicholas myth by the Catholics. One of the powers Odin had was the ability to 'speak things into being'.

Santa Claus' power shifted from Christian to being personal power. It was he, not Odin, or Poseidon, or Jesus, but Santa himself that called the shots. As a newly formed magic power in his own right, Santa found that he no longer needed a lot of the Christian trappings. Gone was Saint Peter's Book of Life, Santa now had his own magical 'list' which he could refer to anytime to find out who was 'naughty or nice'. (This, I think, explains the Plasticine). St. Nick's entire life changed from there on in. Suddenly, he was free to do as he wished, unshackled by the need to fit it all into Christian lore.

Let's take a look at what he did with all of these newfound magical powers...

Reindeer

Between William Gilley's poem and the proliferation of Moore's 'Night before Christmas', Santa managed to corral for himself a total of eight reindeer.. They are: Donner, Dasher, Cupid, Comet, Blitzen,

Vixen, Prancer, and Dancer. (That's not listed in the traditional order, but hey , be impressed. I wrote that out from memory.) For the most part these names are pretty basic, with the exception of Donner and Blitzen.

All the names of the reindeer were invented by Moore, who obviously understood some of the true origins of the Saint Nicholas character he wrote about. You see, Donner and Blitzen are archaic Norse words meaning Thunder and Lightning, an obvious allusion to Odin, who controlled these elements. (Note: They're also used in modern German. i.e.: "Blitz" means lightning, as in the Blitzkrieg, meaning "sudden attack.")

Using his magic powers, Santa Claus forced these poor, innocent, sweet and gentle creatures into an eternity of slave labor, flying his fat ass around the globe at top speeds. This, you'll recall, is a trick he obviously learned from Old Nick, the devil of Scandinavia.

Santa's Magic Sack

You'll recall that St. Nick had bequeathed his magic sack to Black Pete a few hundred years earlier when he gave up on the idea of dragging kids off to Hell in it. Well, it seems it was left behind by a disgruntled Black Pete after he was fired by the Corporate marketing companies. Since Santa had forgotten all about the torturing little kids part of his job, he decided he could still use its magical properties to bring gifts to every kid on the planet. As the magic properties of this sack allowed him to carry in it the entire inventory of Toys'R'Us, it was a welcome addition to the North American Christmas tale.

Elves

The elves thing came from Scandinavia, where elves and gnomes are still part of the popular culture today. (We also get the idea of garden gnomes from them). The media, in their frantic quest to fulfill the public' need for anything Christmas related, dug up some of the old Scandinavian tales at one point. In them, St. Nicholas hung around with a lot of magical figures, including elves. When this idea hit the States the people who were pumping out reams of Christmas fiction at the time were happy to latch on to this new addition to the tale. Suddenly Santa Claus had helpers up there at the North Pole.

While this came from Scandinavia, which is ostensibly Protestant, the addition of the elves to Santa Claus lore in North America is a testament to his non-Christian magical powers. The beings he hangs around with are all considered evil and satanic by most Christians. Cute as they may be, elves are still unnatural minions of the Devil. Not unlike the Easter Bunny, who's quite obviously a 'Pooka' (a large, anthropomorphized forest creature from Celtic myth).

Holly and Ivy and Mistletoe

Now, we all know that holly and Ivy are the male and female in Celtic and Norse lore, and that the intertwining of these two plants represents the sexual union. Santa, with his new powers (obviously bestowed upon him by 'G' rated marketing people) magically transformed the holly and ivy to represent... green stuff. Just green stuff. No sexual references there, just plain, old green stuff that looks pretty and smells nice.

No longer imbued with sexual power from Frigga, Santa Claus and Co. transformed this powerful aphrodisiac into the contemporary obligatory kiss. The bastards.

Fruitcake

Originally, a heavy sickly sweet concoction weighing no less than five pounds, not even the new found magical powers of Santa could transform this abomination into anything better than simple cannon fodder. (Okay... it used to represent the bounty of Ops, goddess of agriculture in Rome. It now represents the vile depths to which the culinary arts can sink.)

Christmas Tree/ Christmas Lights

Once the symbol of the sun in the Saturnalia festivals in Rome and the Odin festivals in Norway, Santa magically transformed the Christmas light to a symbol of hope and prosperity for Hydro companies everywhere.

This one goes all the way back to Attis, that god in Asia-minor we talked about in the Virgin Birth game. He's the earliest record that I know of people honoring a tree. Attis was sacrificed on one (and, hey, so was Jesus... and Mithras... as was Odin. You'd figure the various apostles would learn to keep their messiahs away from trees). Anyway, the Old Testament tells you NOT to have a Christmas tree. (I already gave you the Biblical reference earlier... Jeremiah 10 verse 3. Geez...work with me here people...)

The Druids used to bury their dead beneath a sapling and honor the tree. Then there's the Bonsai Tree in Japan that's worshipped because it represents the souls of all departed ancestors. (I know... the Japanese thing has absolutely no bearing on the Christmas story at all and it's a real stretch to try throw in it in a Christmas book. I only mention it because a friend of mine was really drunk in Japan once and, being Canadian, did what he felt was appropriate when drunk: he found a tree to piss behind. As it turned out it was the family Bonsai Tree, representing the honor and respect of his host family for centuries back. My friend doesn't go to Japan much anymore).

Ok, suffice to say trees had always been a sacred and holy thing except in Judaism, Christianity, and State of Washington. When the tree became a popular Christmas symbol (around 1800) there was an attempt at a cover story for why Christians would have a tree, but it was pretty thin. The story goes that Saint Boniface, knowing that Christmas trees were non-Christian, chopped down a huge oak that was Heathenishly decorated. It fell, crushing every tree around it except for a little fir tree. He interpreted the survival of this one tree as a sign from God that the fir tree was ok to decorate, so he added the evergreen to the Christian Christmas myth. It was a pretty thin excuse for going against the Biblical precedent, and few people actually bought into it.

Enter: American Santa. Using his magical powers the American Santa somehow managed to convince modern Christian's that even though their own book tells them not to have a Christmas Tree, they NEEDED a place under which to stuff the myriad of presents "Santa" would be bringing them. To add insult to injury, Santa also managed to convince them that it was a good idea to shove the top of the tree up the butt of an angel, presumably the same Angel that inspired Jeremiah to nix the Christmas tree idea.

Ok...suffice to say that the new Santa Claus pretty much dropped any kind of Christian ties Christmas might have had before 1900. If it could have been done the holiday would likely have been renamed 'Cashmas' but for some odd reason the marketing guys decided to employ some subtlety. Besides, they kinda had to leave the Baby Jesus something, it being Christmas and all...

It's a Wonderful Life

Okay, we've already discussed the whole Scrooge concept, so I won't bother dragging it up again. I'll leave that to NBC. But I think it's apt that I take aim at It's a Wonderful Life and Miracle on 49th Street; two seminal hallmarks in the theatrical milieu of this neo-Christmas genre. (Okay... I admit it. I only wrote that sentence to prove that I really do know big words). I'm willing to bet that one or both of these movies are currently being aired as you're reading this book. I salute your taste.

The whole reason I bring them up is that both movies are nails in the coffin of the Christian Christmas. Sure, they leave you feeling like everything is warm and loving and beautiful, but if you check the scripts you'll notice that nowhere in either movie is the name Jesus or Christ mentioned. Not that that's a bad thing mind you, but I figure I should point out that even the illusion of a religious justification for the holiday basically evaporated about this time. Let me show ya what I mean...

In Miracle on 49th Street, one Kris Kringle (obviously a German Christ-child) claims to be Santa Claus. As he's working as a Santa Claus in Gimbals Department store, this might all seem rather fortuitous for everyone concerned. But as these cheesy, Hollywood movie scripts tend to go, it all blows up and Kris Kringle winds up in court having to defend his identity. He is defended by a young and bright attorney who decides to prove that Kris Kringle really is THE Santa Claus. If you want the details on how all this went down, just turn to channel 7, 11, 36, 47, or 65 and watch the movie. Suffice to say, the defense proves (as the audience knows all along) that Kris Kringle is indeed Santa Claus, complete with flying reindeer.

In and of itself this is just a movie that affirms the existence of a Santa Claus who endorses gifts (i.e. spending). The thing is, this movie, like Dickens', is played over and over and over and over and... you get the idea. The reason? Its main message is 'gifts are good'. The whole Santa Claus issue is about gift-giving. No Jesus. No God. The movie makes no attempt to give any religious or Christian reason for giving the gifts that Kris Kringle endorses throughout the movie. It's secular without saying so. The same is true of the other great American Christmas classic, It's a Wonderful Life.

In It's a Wonderful Life, Jimmy Stewart tries to commit suicide but is stopped by a bumbling wingless angel named Clarence. Throughout the movie, Clarence talks to God without using His name. In the end, Jimmy Stewart decides he wants to live and Clarence gets his wings. It's enough to send you into insulin shock. Nowhere in the story, though, does Jimmy Stewart, his wife, the pharmacist, or any of his siblings even refer to Jesus as being connected in any way, shape or form, to the Christmas story. Again, the message at the end is one of 'giving'.

One of the clearest examples of this subtext in the movie is in the scene where Clarence and Stewart are sitting in a bar.

The cash register is being opened and closed, making a ringing sound. Clarence (for no apparent reason) says "Every time a bell rings an angel gets his wings." Superficially, this is supposed to mean that angels were being rewarded for their efforts, so Clarence is happy. The visual image is striking however; an angel dancing at the sound of a cash register ringing over and over.

In the final scene, Jimmy Stewart stands next to a huge Christmas tree with tons of money and presents donated to him by the people of the town. Like Dickens' tale, the money and gifts given become the focal point of the holiday. Not Jesus. Not God. Not even Clarence, the only preternatural being in the story. The moral is GIVE. The message is SPEND.

I find that it's only people with little or no education that actually believe the Jesus-Christmas connection. I've never encountered a priest or minister that would actually contend that the classic Christian claim to the holiday was sound. They know about the Saturnalia festivals etc.. It's kind of hard to get a Catholic to admit that the Virgin Birth story was adopted myth, but for the most part ministers will at least agree that it was probably "allegorical". The laity, however, tend to want to kill you for questioning the holy and perfect word of God Almighty, though they tend to ignore things like Genesis 2:25.

And The Underachiever of the Year Award Goes To...

The Grinch.

I had such hope for this guy. I mean, he worked hard, struggled against huge odds, and in the end failed miserably. I always get choked up and teary eyed when I see how low the guy sunk, actually carving up the roast beast for those annoying little Who's down in Whoville.

Let me set the record clear on what's actually going on in this animated flick. Ostensibly, the message of this cartoon is that even when the Grinch took away all the presents and food and Christmas trees, the "spirit" of Christmas still existed. The Whos, bereft of all their belongings, still sang and shared in the warmth and love of the Christmas season. Seeing this, the Grinch has a moment of conversion and brings all their stuff back.

Please, allow me to point out a few flaws in this sentiment...

Everyone knows damn well that Christmas is about gifts and marketing. A lot of companies would simply go under if it weren't for the revenues brought in from this holiday. The thing is, no one wants to believe that this is what it's all about. Enter: the Grinch. In the cartoon all the presents and food are stolen and yet the Christmas spirit is still celebrated. But let's not forget that these are Whos, not humans. In real life if this happened the entire day would be ruined. There'd be a lot of anger and crying and flipping out, and everyone involved would agree that they'd been cheated out of their Christmas. There would be no warm, loving moment of communal signing and happy joyous unity. Most likely, they'd order pizza, buy a bottle of booze, and sit around planning the execution of the bastard that stole all their stuff.

But we don't want to believe this is all that Christmas is about. We want to believe there's something deep and mystic and loving beneath all the spending and feasting. This is where little tales like the Grinch comes in. In them we can sit back with all our gifts intact and believe (because Dr. Seuss said so) that if it were all taken away we'd still have that same feeling of warmth and love that comes from getting a new DVD player.

There's a whole genre of these "If it's all taken away we'll still feel love and warmth" type flicks out there now. With them, we can carry on putting ourselves in huge debt trying to buy the "perfect gifts", content in the knowledge that it's not about the gifts. There's a deeper, ineffable meaning to all this spending.

And, in the end, I suppose there is. It's called the Gross National Product.

Suicide: The Modern Christmas Fable

Razors pain you; rivers are damp; acids stain you; and drugs cause cramp. Guns aren't lawful; nooses give; gas smells awful; you might as well live. ~ Dorothy Parker

The vast majority of people just tend to ride out the season these days. Christmas has now become a truly secular holiday, governed for the most part by the advertising and promotions of the merchants and corporations that have created the modern Christmas.

The thing is, people actually have figured this whole scenario out. While they don't have all the facts, there is this growing suspicion that this Christmas thing is a load of crap. This suspicion has led to a new myth about Christmas that I will take great delight in destroying for you.

The modern myth has it that Christmas is the number one suicide time of year. This is based on the idea that people who don't have family and gifts and such are more inclined to off themselves on Christmas because the holiday leaves them alone and lonely. Everyone seems to believe this, and there's a lot of apocryphal data out there to back it up. (i.e.: I "heard somewhere" that there's fifty times as many suicides at Christmas than in the rest of the year combined). For the record, this is simply not true. Here's the real data, quoted from the most exhaustive stats I could find. (These include the New England Journal of Medicine, the Mayo Clinic reports, and the American Medical Association.)

1: A study examining seasonal trends in more than 3,670 suicides and about 3,300 psychiatric admissions to the Veterans Affairs Medical Center in Durham, N.C. found no increase in suicides or psychiatric admissions around the Christmas and New Year's holidays.

2: From a 1995 news article about the holiday season myth:

"Suicide is not linked to holidays, according to Mayo researchers.(sic) A study of all reported suicides in Olmsted County during a 35-year period did not find an excess number of suicides just before, during or after Thanksgiving, Christmas, New Year's or the Fourth of July holidays. Nor did researchers find a higher suicide rate on birthdays, or three days before or after birthdays. However, their work, concluded in 1985, did affirm other studies showing that suicides are most numerous early in the week and least common on weekends."

3: Researchers used National Center for Health Statistics data to check suicide rates on specific holidays over the entire decade of the 1970s. On an average day, there were 34 suicides per million people. Holiday rates were

26 for Thanksgiving, 30 for Christmas and New Year's Eve, and below average on every major holiday expect New Year's Day. The New Year's Day rate rose to 41 per million. Researchers believe the jump occurs because New Year's Day is the end of holiday season, and people get depressed at the prospect of returning to work and everyday life.

4: Psychiatric visits to hospital emergency departments reach their lowest point of the year one to two weeks before Christmas, and other holidays like New Year's Day, Easter and Independence Day. The studies conclude that if holiday depression does descend every December, its effects are too minor or it involves too few people to show up in the official statistics.

The evidence is pretty easy to find. Just go on line or to the library and look up any study regarding suicide rates. You'll see that the points I just listed are indicative of a whole slew of reports and studies done regarding suicide and Christmas. Across the board, the results bear out: the Christmas suicide is a myth. It's not that people don't off themselves at Christmas, it's just not any more or less frequent than at any other time of the year.

Summary

A lot of people have been asking me *Why pick on Christmas?* If that whole suicide statistic is wrong, and everybody makes money off of it, then why bother attacking the happy, ignorant Christian souls that want to celebrate the season in their own way?"

Well, I could tell you that I am merely interested in the education of the masses, and that this book is my attempt to introduce some basic historical facts into the existing myths of Christmas. I would, however, be lying through my teeth. I'm about as philanthropic as Imelda Marcos, and those that know me would readily see through this lie.

I could just say I'm doing it for the money, but that's a rather flat answer as well. Were it simply that I'd use my religious knowledge to come up with something more akin to "Chicken Soup for the Heathenous Soul".

The truth is that I basically just got fed up. I finally got to the point where I'd seen one too many manger scenes with wise men and Santa Claus in them and decided I had to either take a high powered rifle to the lot of them, or write a book explaining how idiotic these supposedly "historical" Christmas tales are. As I'd promised the judge after that whole Easter Bunny incident that I'd never do the high powered rifle thing again, I opted to write a book.

It's just frustrating as hell to know the origins of all this stuff and still have to put up with listening to glassy-eyed Christians berate me every Christmas for not knowing "the true Reason for the Season." If you try to mention the Saturnalia festivals or the Norse and Celtic origins of all this stuff they insist that you're missing the point. Somehow, despite every historical record you can present, they still insist that Christmas was when Jesus was born, that St. Nicholas was a divine messenger, that it's the power of the Christian word that keeps this season alive, and if you run fast enough and hard enough, the wall opposite the elevator won't stop you from reaching the lawn.

Having explained the origins of all these myths, I think I can now say with relative impunity that the success of the Christmas myth has little if anything to do with Jesus. The Christianity tie in was developed in the fourth century, and was at its height, only marginally accepted into the Yule tradition. Christmas was originally about Saturn, Odin, and Poseidon. Eventually guys like Holt Nickar and the Celtic Yule Father got tied in. Catholicism adopted and used all this to increase its power as a hegemony, but made no real attempt to hide the Celtic, Norse, and Scandinavian origins of the myth.

Eventually, when all the religions were done with it, Christmas died for a couple centuries until it was revived by industry and commerce in the 1800's.

That's it. No manger, no star of Bethlehem. Christians in particular want to mourn the loss of Jesus as the focal point of the Christmas season, unaware that he was never the reason for the existence of the holiday to begin with.

For you, the reader, I hope this book can act as a sort of "War on Christmas" field manual, designed to give you a quick, ready response to the barrage of tinsel, lights, candy canes, and manger scenes that invade our streets, shops, and TV stations every December. (Wow... a lot of commas in that sentence...)

A friend of mine has a sign on his door that I quite like. I have no idea where the inscription comes from, though I'd happily give credit to whoever wrote it. It seems to me to be the perfect quote upon which to end this book.

The sign, written in bold red with a white background, simply reads:

"Chaos, panic, & disorder - my work here is done. "

Sincerely,
Your ever-so-humble author and narrator,

Wm. Hopper
.

Bibliography

U.S. News/Bozell Poll of 1,003 adults conducted by KRC Research Nov. 6-10, 1996, by U.S. News pollsters Celinda Lake of Lake Research and Ed Goeas of the Tarrance Group.

"Retail Outlets are Bracing for Many Unhappy Returns," Washington Post, December 25, 1997.

White Paper (International Council of Shopping Centers, 1998): *Deregulated economies increasing inequality:*

Kevin Phillips, *Politics of Rich and Poor* (New York: Random House, 1990).

"Holiday Blues? Bah, Humbug," Pittsburgh Post-Gazette, December 4, 1995, p. A9.

Emile Durkheim, *The Elementary Forms of Religious Life*, Joseph W. Swain, trans. (Glencoe, IL.: Free Press, 1954 [original 1912]).

Earl W. Count, *4,000 Years of Christmas* (New York: Henry Schuman, 1948), republished in 1997 by Ulysses Press

Richard Heinberg, *Celebrate the Solstice: Honoring the Earth's Seasonal Rhythms* (Wheaton, IL: Quest Books, 1993)

Steven Nissenbaum, *The Battle for Christmas* (New York: Knopf, 1996).

Charles Panbati: *Panati's Extraordinary Origins of Everyday Things* (Harper and Row, 1987)
Clement Moore, *Twas the Night Before Christmas*
The Nag Hammadi Library,
Holy Bible
Apocrapha

Made in the USA
San Bernardino, CA
06 August 2015